D0360041

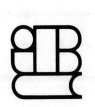

PLANNING RESPONSIBLY FOR ADULT EDUCATION

Ronald M. Cervero
Arthur L. Wilson

PLANNING RESPONSIBLY FOR ADULT EDUCATION

*A Guide to Negotiating
Power and Interests*

Jossey-Bass Publishers · San Francisco

Published by

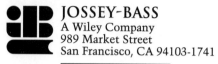

JOSSEY-BASS
A Wiley Company
989 Market Street
San Francisco, CA 94103-1741

www.josseybass.com

Copyright © 1994 by John Wiley & Sons, Inc.

Jossey-Bass is a registered trademark of John Wiley & Sons, Inc.
No part of this publication may be reproduced, stored in a retrieval system, or transmitted in any form or by any means, electronic, mechanical, photocopying, recording, scanning, or otherwise, except as permitted under Sections 107 or 108 of the 1976 United States Copyright Act, without either the prior written permission of the Publisher or authorization through payment of the appropriate per-copy fee to the Copyright Clearance Center, 222 Rosewood Drive, Danvers, MA 01923, (978) 750-8400, fax (978) 750-4744. Requests to the Publisher for permission should be addressed to the Permissions Department, John Wiley & Sons, Inc., 605 Third Avenue, New York, NY 10158-0012, (212) 850-6011E, fax (212) 850-6008, e-mail: permreq@wiley.com.

Jossey-Bass books and products are available through most bookstores. To contact Jossey-Bass directly, call (888) 378-2537, fax to (800) 605-2665, or visit our website at www.josseybass.com.

Substantial discounts on bulk quantities of Jossey-Bass books are available to corporations, professional associations, and other organizations. For details and discount information, contact the special sales department at Jossey-Bass.

We at Jossey-Bass strive to use the most environmentally sensitive paper stocks available to us. Our publications are printed on acid-free recycled stock whenever possible, and our paper always meets or exceeds minimum GPO and EPA requirements.

Jossey-Bass also publishes its books in a variety of electronic formats. Some content that appears in print may not be available in electronic books.

Library of Congress Cataloging-in-Publication Data

Cervero, Ronald M.

Planning responsibly for adult education : a guide to negotiating power and interests / Ronald M. Cervero, Arthur L. Wilson.
p. cm. — (The Jossey-Bass higher and adult education series)
Includes bibliographical references and index.
ISBN 1-55542-628-X
1. Adult education—United States—Planning. I. Wilson, Arthur L., date. II. Title. III. Series.
LC5251.C47 1994
374.73—dc20

93–43174
CIP

FIRST EDITION
HB Printing   10 9 8 7 6 5

Code 9425

The Jossey-Bass
Higher and Adult Education Series

Consulting Editor
Adult and Continuing Education

Alan B. Knox
University of Wisconsin, Madison

To our families:
Janna Dresden, Francesca Cervero, Mark Cervero,
Barbara L. Bryant, and Kaitlin H. Wilson-Bryant

Contents

Preface   xi

The Authors   xvii

**Part One: Understanding
the Practice of Program Planning**   1

1. Practical and Political Dimensions of Planning   3

2. Planning as a Process of Negotiating Interests   13

**Part Two: Negotiating Interests
in Planning Practice: Three Cases**   33

3. Fixing an Organization Through Management
   Education   35

4. Updating Practitioners in University
   Continuing Education   62

5. Promoting Social Change in
   Community-Based Education   88

ix

Part Three: Guidelines for Responsible Planning   115

6.   To Plan Responsibly, Be Political   117

7.   Represent Interests Democratically   137

8.   Develop Skills and Knowledge to
     Negotiate Responsibly   155

9.   Understand Planning as a Social Practice   171

     References   193

     Index   203

Preface

Why does the field of adult education need another book about planning educational programs for adults? Certainly, there is an abundance of theories for planning programs, as well as many books on specific aspects of planning, such as needs assessment, program evaluation, instructional design, administration, and management. Yet most practitioners consider that books about planning, even the best ones, go only partway toward capturing what it means to act responsibly in the world. Advice on how to plan is given, these practitioners say, as if the world in which they must plan were devoid of disagreeable people, nasty politics, and concern about the economic bottom line. Thus, planners feel they are walking through quicksand and are getting advice about characteristic land formations instead of a rope. Practitioners' skepticism is probably well founded, for much that has been written about planning has focused on technical, "how to" skills while presupposing some ideally neutral staging area in which these skills will be exercised and has remained surprisingly silent on the troublesome issues of "what for" and "for whom."

Practitioners will tell you that theories do not plan programs, people do. This incredibly obvious point forms the core of our book. Taking people-planning as the thing to understand and improve immediately draws attention to two central realities that must be accounted for. First, whenever people are acting in an organizational context, they act within relationships of power in order to carry out their work. As every experienced planner knows, the context for program planning is not always marked by consensus and cooperation in political relationships. More often, planners must negotiate between conflicting interests in an arena where the power relationships are asymmetrical and complex. Regardless of whether the political relationships are marked by consensus or conflict and of whether they are symmetrical or asymmetrical, however, the politics of the situation always matters in responsible planning. This observation brings us to the second reality that must constantly be taken into account: planners must know how to act responsibly within relationships of power. If people always plan in the face of power, to whom are they responsible for the educational programs they construct? Which people get to decide the purposes, content, and format of the program? Is it always the people who have the most power? Is it the adults who will participate in the program, the leadership of the institution that is sponsoring the program, the people who will teach in the program, or the planners themselves? These questions cannot be answered simply in light of the situation itself; rather, they require the planner to hold clearly defined beliefs about how to act responsibly in the face of power.

We have written the book in response to these two realities of program planners' practice. Nearly all models for planning programs for adults have treated power, politics, and ethics as noise that gets in the way of good planning; in so doing, these models set up dichotomies between rationality and politics or, more generally, between individual planners and the social structures within which they act. Our effort here is based on the assumption that far from being noise, power relationships structure the terrain on which programs are always planned and on which planners must always act. And while people must have technical knowledge and skill in order to plan well, these are not enough. We argue that ethical vision coupled with political knowledge and skill are necessary to plan responsibly for the education of adults.

Purpose and Organization of the Book

In this book, we offer adult educators a practical and ethical guide to planning practice. On the basis of the real-world experience of actual program planners, we argue that planning is a social activity, in which adult educators routinely negotiate personal and organizational interests to construct educational programs. The form and content of any educational program are expressly a function of who negotiates what interests in what context. Because planning is a social (rather than an individual) activity, it is important to understand planners' interaction with their organizational settings. In *Planning Responsibly for Adult Education,* therefore, we assume that power and interests are central to action and ask what adult educators can do to plan programs responsibly. We explore how program planners can anticipate the structural relationships of power in which they must necessarily act and how they can then respond in ways that nurture, though hardly ensure, a democratic planning process. This is not a procedural account of how to plan programs, although we believe that adult educators need technical information and skill to plan responsibly. Rather, it is our attempt to make sense of program planning practice in a way that honors its situation-specific character as well as its fundamentally ethical basis. We hope to enlarge adult educators' sense of responsibility and at the same time offer them practical guides for looking at the world in which they must necessarily carry out their responsibilities.

We are directly concerned with adult educators' planning "practice" and make our essential argument in the first eight chapters. The discussion of theory appears in Chapter Nine and is necessary only for readers who want to better understand the intellectual roots, both in adult education and in the social sciences, of our effort to develop a theory of program-planning practice in adult education. In Chapter Nine, we explain why adult education (and therefore program-planning practice) is a social rather than a scientific activity—and place the claim in the context of similar theoretical explanations of other forms of human activity. Thus, while we certainly use program-planning theory throughout, the book is not *about* theory, except for the last chapter.

In Part One, we draw readers' attention to the importance of program-planning practice in adult education (Chapter One) and offer a model of what adult educators actually do when planning programs (Chapter Two). The model, which presents negotiating interests as what really matters in practice, is the bedrock on which the remainder of the book is built. In Chapter Two, we review three other models of planning (which we call the classical, naturalistic, and critical viewpoints) and show how our model further develops important elements of all three viewpoints.

The three chapters in Part Two show how the concept of negotiating interests can be used both to make sense of the empirical realities that planners face daily and to account for the way educational programs are actually constructed. The three chapters focus on different types of organizational settings, including a business (Chapter Three), a higher education institution (Chapter Four), and a social action agency (Chapter Five). Each case is organized in the same way, with an introduction to the planners and their organizational contexts, an analysis of the interests under negotiation, and a final section showing how negotiation about the interests directly produced the actual program and affected its purposes, audience, content, and format. The chapters in this part do more than verify for readers the value of the negotiation model. We believe that explicit identification of the interests offers adult educators a practical way to examine their own planning efforts, and we urge them to conduct similar analyses of their own planning practices.

After demonstrating in the first two parts that negotiating interests is the central activity of planning practice, in Part Three we move to the practical question of what adult educators can do to plan responsibly. We offer an approach to planning practice that illuminates questions of "how to" by articulating a political and ethical sense of "what for." We ask what rational action would look like if planning practice were seen as negotiating interests in the context of varying relationships of power. Our answer is that rational action requires anticipating how existing relationships of power are likely to support or constrain a substantively democratic planning process and then acting in ways to nurture such a process. Thus when educators plan a program, they should have a clear understanding of the social context, power relationships, and interests through which the program is being constructed (Chapter Six), a commitment to involve in the planning the people (or their representatives) who have a legitimate interest in the program (Chapter Seven), and a repertoire of technical, political, and ethical understanding, to negotiate responsibly when constructing the program (Chapter Eight).

Audience

We have written *Planning Responsibly for Adult Education* in response to our own need to better understand how planning practice shapes the world in which we live. We believe the major audience is educators who work with and plan programs for adults. The book is primarily about the everyday world of planners who include, but are not limited to, continuing educators in colleges and universities, community educators and organizers, literacy educators, human resource specialists and trainers in business and industry, labor and union educators, continuing educators in the professions, and educators in social movements. In short, the book is intended for anyone who has some responsibility for planning education for adults in an organization or a community. The second audience we hope to reach comprises educators, either experienced or just starting out in practice, who are pursuing advanced degrees in adult education or related fields, as well as our colleagues who teach planning courses in graduate programs. We hope that in the luxury of advanced study, practitioners can take time out to reflect and then act on the ideas we propose in the book. We firmly believe that the book offers planners in the field a language with which to talk about things they already know but have had no systematic way of discussing. We believe that by becoming articulate in this language, and by better understanding what really matters in planning, educators can improve planning practice, and therefore adult education as a whole.

Acknowledgments

The book could not have been constructed without the assistance of many collaborators and commentators. We must thank Lynn Luckow now president of Jossey-Bass, and Alan B. Knox, the consulting editor, who encouraged us to proceed with the book during our early discussions in the fall of 1989. Subsequently, Alan and Gale Erlandson, senior editor of the Jossey-Bass Higher and Adult

Education Series, offered much constructive advice about the overall shape of the manuscript. We owe our greatest debt and deepest thanks to the planners whose practice activities form the core of the book: "Pete" and "Joan"; "Carl," "Bob," and "Richard"; and "Marti" and "Ann" (whose real names have been disguised in the interests of preserving privacy). Without their openness to our intrusions, their frankness in our many conversations, and their genuine spirit of inquiry and reflection, we would be much less certain about the ideas presented in the book. Through his untiring efforts to acquaint us with many exciting writers in the field of social theory, David Little opened a colossal door when he introduced us to John Forester, whose work gave us the language for understanding what planners really do. Forester is an urban planner and policy analyst; he showed us how to talk practically about theory and theoretically about practice. His work has been a constant inspiration, and without it we would not have been able to develop a politically astute and ethically illuminating understanding of planning in adult education. We have especially appreciated Von Pittman's insightful comments, for it was his insistent concern about the lack of correspondence between planning theory and planning practice that has inspired us. Joseph Donaldson and Karen Watkins used the manuscript in their program-planning courses and offered us an indication of how the book might be used in graduate education. We learned a great deal about what we could say and what we needed to say from Pamela Kleiber and David Mills, who read early drafts of the three case studies. As always, the editorial staff at Jossey-Bass has been helpful throughout the editorial process. Finally, we need to thank all the participants in our graduate courses over the past four years who have read and commented on the cases and ideas in the book during its formative stages. They gave us the opportunity to talk, so that we could hear what we had to say about planning educational programs for adults.

December 1993   Ronald M. Cervero
                                                                       Athens, Georgia

                                                                       Arthur L. Wilson
                                                                       Muncie, Indiana

The Authors

Ronald M. Cervero is professor in the Department of Adult Education at the University of Georgia. He received his B.A. degree (1973) from St. Michael's College (Vermont) in psychology, his A.M. degree (1975) from the University of Chicago in the social sciences, and his Ph.D. degree (1979), also from the University of Chicago, in adult education.

Cervero has been a program planner in many settings, including community colleges, professional associations, and higher education. He has served as chair of the North American Adult Education Research Conference (1983), as cofounder of the Midwest Research-to-Practice Conference in Adult and Continuing Education (1982), as member of the executive committee of the Commission of Professors of Adult Education (1986-1988), and as coeditor for *Adult Education Quarterly* (1988-1993). He has been a visiting faculty member at other universities, including the University of Tennessee, the University of British Columbia, Pennsylvania State University, and the University of Wisconsin, Madison. He has published many book chapters and research articles in the areas of adult literacy education and continuing professional education. His book *Effective Continuing Education for Professionals* (1988) received the 1989 Cyril O. Houle World Award for Literature in Adult Education from the American Association for Adult and Continuing Education and the 1990 Frandson Award for Literature in the Field of Adult Education from the National University Continuing Education Association.

Arthur L. Wilson is assistant professor of adult and community education in the Department of Educational Leadership at Ball State University. He received his B.A. degree (1972) from the University of Virginia in sociology, his M.S.Ed. degree (1980) from Virginia Polytechnic Institute and State University in adult and continuing education, and his Ed.D. degree (1991) from the University of Georgia in adult education.

His program-planning experience includes curriculum development and teacher training in local literacy programs, staff development projects for statewide literacy, state association conference and professional development, a national program of professional training and certification, and graduate program development in adult education. He served on the executive board of the Virginia Association for Adult and Continuing Education (1986–1988) and received its distinguished service award (1987). He received a Kellogg Fellowship (1988–1990) to attend the University of Georgia and received the Graduate Student Research Award (1992) given by the North American Adult Education Research Conference. He was the editorial associate for *Adult Education Quarterly* (1988–1991) and is consulting editor for *Adult Education Quarterly* and *Adult Basic Education*. In addition to program planning, his work has focused on the foundations of adult education, continuing education for the professions, and adult learning. He has published articles in *Adult Education Quarterly* and the *International Journal of Lifelong Education* and chapters in edited collections. He has been an adjunct or visiting faculty member at Old Dominion University, George Mason University, and the University of Alberta, Canada.

PLANNING RESPONSIBLY FOR ADULT EDUCATION

PART 1

Understanding
the Practice
of Program Planning

Part One asks how it is possible to understand what program planners in adult education really do and what matters in their practice. Chapter One makes the argument, which carries throughout the book, that to improve practice, the focus of attention must be on the practical and political character of planning. The middle part of the chapter describes how we organized and conducted our study of planning practice in adult education. This chapter ends by explaining what this approach to program planning can hope to accomplish. Chapter Two describes three major traditions in the literature of adult education and the general field of curriculum that have been used to describe what program planners really do and what matters in their practice (which we call the *classical, naturalistic,* and *critical viewpoints*). We identify the important contributions that these three viewpoints make in developing a new model for understanding planning practice. This model, which has planners negotiating interests within social relationships of power in order to construct educational programs, forms the basis upon which the remainder of the book rests.

ONE

Practical and
Political Dimensions
of Planning

The educational programs fashioned through educators' planning practices for adult education address many practical problems facing society. With these programs, for example, planners attempt to improve the quality of the business enterprises in which they work, to strengthen the capacities of teachers in U.S. educational systems, to revitalize citizens' involvement in the governing of states and the nation, and to address racism and sexism in social relationships. The very existence of these programs affects the world. Of course, all educational planners believe the world will be a better place because of their efforts. Thus, much is at stake in attempting to understand not only how planners' practices shape educational programs but also what planners can do to recognize problems and seize opportunities. Most theories directed at improving practice see program planners as problem solvers who should rigorously apply principles in their practice; the organizational and social contexts are seen as noise that impedes application of the principles. As Apps (1979) points out, these principles have a familiar five-step structure: (1) assessing learners' needs, (2) defining objectives based on these needs, (3) identifying learning experiences to meet those objectives, (4) organizing those learning experiences, and (5) evaluating the program in terms of the objectives. The planning literature has repeated this structure for so long that theorists see it as the sine qua non of good program planning. In some ways, this is a truly comforting approach—it tells planners to follow the same principles, regardless of the organizational context. Yet most people who must actually plan programs claim that, far from being noise, the context always matters as they attempt to plan well, and it seriously affects their planning efforts. A truly practical theory, then, must offer planners not only a set of technical procedures but also a way to understand the organizational contexts in which the procedures are to be carried out.

The central claim of the book is that planning programs is a social activity in which people negotiate personal and organizational interests. The educational programs constructed through these practices do not just appear fully formed on a brochure or in a classroom. Rather, they are planned by real people in complex organizations that have sets of historical traditions, relationships of power, and human needs and interests. The planners construct educational programs from the judgments they make in this messy everyday world. In our view, the struggles that occur in everyday practice are part of the terrain in which educational opportunities for adults are provided. Any account of educational program planning must face these struggles, and few, if any, adult educators would deny they exist. This should not be surprising, for as Forester (1989) points out, planning while "ignoring the opportunities and dangers of an organizational setting is like walking across a busy intersection with one's eyes closed" (p. 7). However, these realities have rarely been taken as a source of insight for theories of program planning.

By focusing on planning practice rather than planning theory, *Planning Responsibly for Adult Education* necessarily attempts to make sense of the noise of organizational and social contexts. All planners know they are not free agents able to translate their own interests directly into the purposes, content, and format of a program. Rather, their planning is always conducted within a complex set of personal, organizational, and social relationships of power among people who may have similar, different, or conflicting sets of interests regarding the program. The planners' responsibility, and the central problem of their practice, center on how to negotiate the interests of these people to construct a program. *Webster's Third New International Dictionary* (1976) defines *responsi-*

ble as "able to answer for one's conduct or obligation, politically answerable." The problem is to answer this question in every concrete planning activity: To whom is the adult educator ethically and politically answerable? Or, stated differently, whose interests will be negotiated in what ways in constructing the educational program? Our answer is that the planner is responsible for negotiating the interests of all people who may be affected by the educational program. This belief in a substantively democratic planning process is based on the long history of democracy in this country and the continuing efforts to structure social relationships according to democratic principles. Our point is simple: if this principle forms the basis of social life in all other domains of society, it should guide the actions of educators of adults. At the same time, it is essential to recognize that educators of adults must always act in historically developing and structurally organized relationships of power, which may either constrain or enable them to negotiate the interests of all people affected. If planners have good intentions but are not politically astute, they are likely to become martyrs or saints, not responsible educators.

In sum, planning practice matters in adult education because the programs will make the world a different place. After all, people with particular sets of interests will have planned the programs. They will have selected certain purposes, content, audiences, and formats for the programs, thereby closing off other possibilities. Each educational program, then, makes a statement about the way the world ought to be. This is not a startling revelation; all other systems constructed by people with particular sets of interests, including capitalism, democracy, and the private health care system, are based on sets of beliefs about the way the world ought to be organized. Simply put, adult education cannot be a neutral activity; if it were, why would anyone care about it? Therein lies educators' central responsibility—namely, what kind of world will their practice shape?

Sources of Insight and Inspiration

Planning educational programs for adults takes a variety of forms and occurs in a wide range of organizations. Throughout the book, we use *planners* as shorthand for a broad array of people who are involved in deliberating about the purposes, content, audience, and format of educational programs for adults. This includes, among others, administrators and program or curriculum developers in for-profit and nonprofit businesses, community agencies, and public schools and higher education institutions. The daily experiences of these people and their knowledge are infinitely more complex than any theory of program planning can fully account for. Yet the realities planners face must be the point of departure for any serious attempt to improve adult education.

This book explores everyday practice in planning programs for adults and assesses its challenges and opportunities. Our central thesis is that planning must be seen as a social activity in which educators negotiate personal and organizational interests. In this view, planners could significantly improve the quality of education by learning how to anticipate and deal with such interests. Our belief in this thesis has deep roots in our own program-planning experience. Each of us has spent much of the past twenty years working in and consulting with a variety of agencies involved in the education of adults, such as community-based and school-based adult literacy programs, state and national professional associations, universities and other postsecondary institutions, and for-profit and nonprofit organizations. Although the literature on educational program planning offered us numerous principles of good practice, such as assessing the needs of the audience, the principles did not seem to account for the important things we have done while planning programs. In many ways, these principles sold our practice short. For example, our judgments about whether or how to assess the needs of our audience depended on a number of factors, including the values and interests of others involved, organizational and interpersonal power relationships, available resources, and a knowledge of the history of planning efforts in the given situation. Thus, as we reflected on our own experiences and those of others, we thought it important to try to account for the political richness, ethical dilemmas, and practical judgments of planning practices.

Those who plan programs on a daily basis lend validity to our observations. In a recent article, Pittman (1989) argues that "graduate programs could improve their image and utility to practitioners by giving serious, considered, scholarly attention to some of the problems and challenges their students will encounter when they enter continuing education" (p. 30). He explains that practitioners must deal regularly with political and economic issues, topics that much of the planning literature considers irrelevant to good program design. For instance, he says that "regardless of how educationally sound or socially desirable a program may be, no program that consistently loses money is well designed" (p. 30). Yet theoretical writings about program planning in adult education rarely address this issue.

Although an important source for the material we present is our personal experience in educational program planning, another source has been the scholarly literature. Others involved in adult education have recently voiced similar concerns about the incompleteness of the program-planning literature (Millar, 1989; Usher and Bryant, 1989). Brookfield (1986) noted that the conventional program-planning models are generally treated with a great deal of skepticism, especially by those with "years of experience dealing with organizations in which personality conflicts, political factors, and budgetary constraints alter neatly conceived plans of action" (p. 202). These practitioners indicate that "they are unable to recognize themselves in the pages of most program development manuals" (Brookfield, 1986, p. 206). In their comprehensive review of the literature on planning programs for adults, Sork and Caffarella (1989) conclude that there are "shortcomings in the planning literature that need to be addressed. Building a theory that takes into account the exigencies of day-to-day responsibilities of practitioners" (p. 243) must be undertaken if planning theories are to be viewed seriously.

This recent questioning of the founding principles of program planning in adult education is similar to a movement that has been under way for twenty-five years in the field of curriculum planning for schools. The clarion call was issued by Schwab (1969): "The field of curriculum is moribund, unable by its present methods and principles to continue its work and desperately in search of new and more effective principles and methods. . . . There will be a renewed capacity to contribute to the quality of American education only if the bulk of curriculum energies are diverted from the theoretic to the practical. . . . It is the discipline concerned with choice and action" (p. 1). Since that time, the field of school-based curriculum planning has been deeply involved in teasing out the implications of turning away from the conventional planning theories (Atkins, 1986; Beyer and Apple, 1988; Cornbleth, 1988).

Much of our inspiration and many insights for the book came from literature outside education. In particular, a variety of professional fields (Schön, 1983, 1987, 1991; Shulman, 1987) and the social sciences (Bernstein, 1983; Dreyfus and Dreyfus, 1986; Lave, 1988) have turned toward understanding everyday practice. For example, by examining actual protocols of practice, Schön has offered an account of how professional practitioners make judgments in their everyday work. Based on an intensive study of nurses working with patients, Benner (1984) presents "the limits of formal rules and calls attention to the discretionary judgment used in actual clinical situations" (p. xix). Our intent was to use the resources of this tradition to understand program-planning practice in adult education. As important as these practice theories have been to planners, however, they generally have lacked an account of the social-structural relationships of power that are central to understanding planning practice in adult education. For this, we turned to the literature of critical social theory in the social sciences (Forester, 1989, 1993; Isaac, 1987), education (Apple, 1990), and adult education (Griffin, 1983; Hart, 1990; Welton, 1987). As Chapters Six through Nine make clear, we found Forester's work particularly helpful in connecting social-structural views of the world with accounts of practice.

Methods

The third source of insight and inspiration came from our intensive observation of the planning practices of several educators of adults. Because of our personal experiences in planning, we believed it would be necessary to keep our account of planning practice empirical. For this reason, we sought people responsible for planning programs for three different types of organizations and asked to observe their planning activities for an upcoming educational program. In selecting the three people, we were less concerned with whether they were "average" than with the fact that they represented recognizable versions of planning practice. We were not primarily concerned with whether the program was a success; rather, our intent was to explore the relationships among the interests affecting planning and the purposes, content, audience, and format of the resultant program.

We selected programs in organizations in which the educational function serves different purposes, thus presenting the planners with different types of tasks. In the first case, we observed Pete and Joan, the planners for a management education program at the Phoenix Company (see Chapter Three). The manifest purpose of the program was to address an organizational problem, the communication between the different levels of the company's management structure. Pete and Joan had worked with the sixty-five participants every day for several years and thus were personally acquainted with all members of the audience. There was no marketing problem—the program was mandated, and the audience was completely prescribed. Pete and Joan experienced the program's effect—or lack of effect—firsthand in the weeks and months after the program was instituted. In the second case, Carl, Bob, and Richard, who work in the College of Pharmacy at State University, planned a continuing education program (see Chapter Four). The manifest purpose of the program was to disseminate the latest university-based research about cardiovascular disease to a statewide population of practicing pharmacists. The planners had no way of knowing which one hundred or so of the six thousand pharmacists in the target audience would attend the program; experience suggested that the topic of the program would determine actual attendance. This was important because the costs of the program had to be recovered from registration fees. In the third case, the primary planner was Marti, a newly hired program coordinator for an agency [Organization for Persons with Disabilities (OPD)] with a social action agenda (see Chapter Five). She wanted her program to help employers understand ways of implementing new federal legislation, the Americans with Disabilities Act, which was designed to prevent discrimination in the workplace against people with disabilities. Like Carl, she did not know which of the 250 members of her target audience of human resource directors would attend.

This presented a marketing problem, because the costs of the program had to be recovered from registration fees.

Each program took four to five months to plan, and two programs were actually conducted; the OPD program was canceled because of insufficient registration a week before its scheduled presentation. The programs were planned and offered (or scheduled, in the OPD case) consecutively; thus, we were never involved in observing the planning of more than one program at the same time. The entire data collection phase lasted two years from the time the planning for the first program began through the final interviews we conducted after completion of the third program. However, in order to mask the identity of the institutions, the time frame within which we have written up the cases in Chapters Three through Five has the programs occurring more or less simultaneously. Given the extraordinary level of access to the planning process needed to collect the data, we sought educators with whom we had an established relationship. We were personally acquainted with the primary planners (Pete, Carl, and Marti) for the three programs. Since we wanted to mask their identity, all names used in the book are fictitious. The planners (Pete and Joan, Bob and Carl, Marti and Ann) have also read their respective chapters and have attested to the accuracy of the descriptions presented.

We collected the data upon which the three cases are based by using observations, interviews, and analyses of documents related to the planning process. Our intent was to sit in on all meetings in which two or more people were involved and to regularly interview the planners to stay abreast of their other activities (such as phone calls and informal, spontaneous conversations). For each program, we asked to observe any planning meetings that were held. We audiotaped the meetings, and at least one of us was present. We then interviewed the principal planners for thirty to forty-five minutes as soon as possible after the meeting and asked them to comment on their judgments about the program. If both of us were present at the planning meeting, the debriefing typically occurred immediately upon its conclusion. Because the planning meetings were scheduled at times convenient for the organization, and often at the last minute, it was not possible for both of us to attend each meeting. In these instances, one would attend and the other would listen to the audiotape. Within a week, we would debrief the principal planners about the meeting. In addition to the interviews keyed to the planning meetings, we conducted several others with the planners to capture judgments that were being made outside the public meetings. Finally, we interviewed the planners within a week after the program had actually been offered in order to learn whether they had changed the original plan and to have them reflect on the entire planning process. We also examined such available planning documents as meeting agendas, program objectives, institutional mission statements, and marketing materials throughout the data collection phase.

We do not claim to be offering in this book either a complete account of planning practice or, it is hoped, the last word on the subject. Rather, we wish to claim a strong plausibility (Forester, 1989) for our interpretation; that is, our arguments can make sense of the everyday world that planners confront when developing educational programs for adults. Although our general aim is to present an analysis of planning practice that is both comprehensive and practical, we do not expect planners to apply it any more than they could apply any other program-planning theory. As the book makes clear, theories do not plan programs; people do. Thus, the certainty that planners often seek in their practice cannot be supplied by planning theories. But neither can practical knowledge or personal values supply this certainty, for we need contributions from all these areas to responsibly plan educational programs for adults. We believe that the theory of planning practice formulated here can contribute to improving adult education. However, it needs to be tested further, and we suggest that its value be assessed according to this criterion: does it help educators of adults recognize more clearly and act more responsibly on the precarious possibilities for politically astute and ethically sensitive planning practice?

So what is new here? By developing an account of practice that assumes that power and interests are central to a planner's action, we hope to draw attention to what educators of adults now do and may do better. We argue that although theories of ethics, power and politics, and program design may be distinguishable in the abstract, they must be integrated in any activity of educational program planning. If we go even partway toward capturing the essential aspects of planning practice and at the same time stimulate others to carry out similar work, we believe these arguments can enrich both our understanding and our practice of planning programs for adults. Our account is not complete, because it complements, rather than substitutes for, other analyses that must be done. We have focused, necessarily, on what is common among planners and contexts. Other analyses might profitably focus on the unique sets of constraints and opportunities, as well as comparative analyses of these factors, presented by certain types of agencies involved in the education of adults. We do not treat systematically the intrapersonal or interpersonal dynamics that often affect planning practices. Nor do we examine in the depth necessary the external relationships that planners form with other agencies in developing programs. We hope that readers of this book are stimulated to carry out further analyses of planning practice.

The next chapter discusses the traditions that educators of adults have used to interpret their practices of program planning. Each tradition comes fully equipped with a language and a set of beliefs about what focus is really important in planning. Chapter Two provides a historical sketch and description of the three major traditions that we believe have been important in shaping our discussions of planning programs for adults. From these traditions, then, grows our own account of planning practice. Our intent in describing program-planning practice as a social activity in which adult educators negotiate interests is to develop a language that reflects what really matters about the actions of adult educators in the everyday world.

TWO

Planning as a Process of Negotiating Interests

If planners are to understand and improve planning practice, an obvious question arises: What do program planners really do? In this chapter, we argue that negotiating interests is central to planning. The process of negotiation can describe what planners do and can suggest ways to recognize problems and seize opportunities in daily practice. The first part of the chapter considers three common accounts of what adult education program planners do (Carr and Kemmis, 1986; Schubert, 1986; Walker and Soltis, 1992) in order to explain why we use negotiation to understand program-planning practice. As part of our analysis, we identify the central insights from each viewpoint that we use to build our own account of planning practice. In the second section, we identify the central problem with all three viewpoints. Each presents a model of practice that strongly emphasizes one or the other sides of the typical dichotomy of planner discretion and structural constraints or, more generally, rationality and politics. We argue that while these dichotomies may be distinguishable in theory, responsible planning practice requires their integration (Forester, 1989; Goodson, 1991). In the final section, we present our view of what planners do and its implications for understanding and improving planning practice.

Three Viewpoints on Planning Practice

The literature offers a number of views of what program planners do. We have distilled these into three common accounts of planning practice, which we label the classical, naturalistic, and critical viewpoints.

The Classical Viewpoint

Anyone wishing to develop educational programs for adults has an abundance of theories from which to draw (Boone, 1985; Knox and Associates, 1980; Langenbach, 1988; Sork and Buskey, 1986). Most see educators of adults as people who apply the principles of these theories to problems they encounter while planning programs. In his classic book about program planning, Knowles (1980) says that before 1950, educators of adults had no theory to support their practice so they relied on intuition. Then books began to appear, including his own *Informal Adult Education* (1950), which extracted from these intuitions principles that could be used by other educators to plan better educational programs. During the subsequent four decades, nearly one hundred more theories about how to plan programs were added to the literature of adult education (Sork and Buskey, 1986). Most were offered on the premise that the curriculum theories used in schools were inappropriate for the situations faced by the educators of adults. Nevertheless, the curriculum development framework presented in Tyler's classic book, *Basic Principles of Curriculum and Instruction* (1949), undergirds most program-planning theories in adult education. Tyler (1949, p. 1) suggests that any curriculum development project should be guided by four questions: What educational purposes should the school seek to attain? What educational experiences can be provided that are likely to attain these purposes? How can the educational experiences be effectively organized? and How can we assess whether the purposes are being attained? Tyler's framework (and the many variants and elaborations, such as Taba, 1962) has been the dominant curriculum theory in education since it was published and is widely considered the classical viewpoint (Posner, 1988; Schubert, 1986). Many educators of adults have noted that the logic of Tyler's framework has also become the classical viewpoint in adult education (Apps, 1979; Brookfield, 1986). Tyler's four questions have been translated into the prescriptive steps of the program-planning process as described in nearly all theories.

The power of the language used in the classical viewpoint is evident when planners describe what they actually do. For example, Knowles (1980, pp. 26–27) asks what educators of adults do. He answers in the language of the classical model:

1. They help learners diagnose their needs for learning.
2. They plan with learners a sequence of experiences that will produce the desired learnings.
3. They create conditions that will cause the learners to want to learn.
4. They select the most effective methods and techniques to produce the desired learnings.
5. They provide the human and material resources necessary to produce the desired learnings.
6. They help the learner measure the outcomes of the learning experiences.

Knowles has not changed the logic of Tyler's questions but rather has been more explicit about the involvement of learners in the process. Any doubt about the dominance of the classical viewpoint was dispelled in one of the few research studies in adult education that has asked program planners how they actually develop programs. Pennington and Green (1976) interviewed fifty-two professional educators and asked them to describe the planning strategies they use every day. From these descriptions, the authors developed a model of the planning process clustered around six types of activities: originating the idea from formal needs assessments and other sources, developing the idea by exploring the extent of interest on the part of people in the field, making a commitment by laying administrative groundwork, developing the program by setting objectives and selecting methods, teaching the course, and evaluating its effect by measuring the results. The logic and language of the model sound familiar because, as the authors conclude, "Planners use the language of the classical model to label their planning actions" (Pennington and Green, 1976, p. 22).

We must ask, however, if this really is what program planners do. Educators might be led to wonder, as Houle (1980) did, whether these fifty-two program planners were "imposing upon the accounts of their own activities some memories of the general patterns that had been described to them" (p. 228). This is surely the case, because the planners themselves claimed not to have used the model in any systematic way. Rather, they stressed the importance of personal values, environmental constraints, and available alternative resources as the critical factors constraining their action in the planning process. Thus, even in the face of describing what is really important in the program-planning processes, the educators could describe what they do only in the vocabulary of the classical viewpoint. Brookfield (1986, p. 206) provides similar evidence that program planners use the language of the classical viewpoint to describe what they do, even as they claim that the viewpoint fails to such a degree to account for the political and economic realities that its practice injunctions cannot be taken seriously. It should not be surprising that the principles of the classical viewpoint do not account for what planners do, because this is not the intention of the authors who construct them. Program-planning theories, according to this viewpoint, tell educators what they ought to do; a theory "describes an idealized process that may or may not fit with the realities of practice" (Sork and Caffarella, 1989, p. 243). The same point has been made for many years about the Tylerian model of curriculum development. Walker (1971) claims that the classical model neglects or distorts important aspects of what really happens as curricula are developed in schools.

Can the classical viewpoint describe what program planners really do? Although this viewpoint has an authoritative and comforting ring to it, real-life planners say that it is not an accurate depiction of what they really have to do and what is important about their everyday practice. They would say that its image—of the educator applying principles to problems—leaves unanswered the crucial questions of who is applying which principles, with what values and interests, and in what organizational setting. Indeed, even theorists who are sympathetic to this viewpoint believe that "anyone who claims that a planning model accurately represents how planning occurs in practice . . . has a naive understanding of what planning involves" (Sork and Caffarella, 1989, p. 234). Thus, although program planners do not simply apply principles to real problems, what they really do is not described.

To be fair, however, these theories were never meant to account for the realities of practice that include the shifting goals, limited resources, relationships of power, and the varying personalities encountered in the everyday world. One reason may be that the audience for these theories is practicing educators, who are assumed to already possess the practical knowledge of these issues that comes from experience. As Knox (1979) explains, "A practitioner's knowledge regarding goals and procedures in the field contributes to proficiency, but must be combined with understanding and experience in actual tasks and roles to produce it" (p. 4). Thus, the theories identify some key questions that must be asked of every educational program (such as its purpose and how its learning experiences can best be organized to meet those purposes) and rely on practitioners' experiential knowledge to answer those questions in practice. Yet they are silent on the matter of exactly how real educators are to answer those questions in the everyday world. What educators should find odd is that, in spite of this silence, most program planners use the language of the classical viewpoint to describe what they do. Critics suggest that educators continue to use this language because they lack the vocabulary to talk about what they do in any other way. Thus, they have pressed for theories that are frankly based on the demands of actual practice.

Where does this analysis leave the classical viewpoint? Although it does not account for the dimensions and variability of planning contexts, the nature of practical judgments, or the values that influence how judgments are made, the classical viewpoint has clearly identified some characteristic questions that must be addressed by any planner. Paraphrasing Tyler, these are, What *purpose(s)* does a program seek? What *content* or educational experiences are likely to attain these purposes? By which *methods* can this content be effectively organized? And, how can these purposes be *evaluated*? It is difficult to imagine a planning situation in which planners' practices do not focus on these questions. However, our theory of planning practice reformulates the way these questions are asked.

The Naturalistic Viewpoint

By shifting our gaze from the idealized principles of the classical viewpoint to actual planning situations, we answer the question,

What do planners do? in a dramatically different way. In the naturalistic viewpoint, educators of adults are no longer planners who apply a standard set of principles and procedures to any situation. Rather, they are real people trying to make judgments about what action to take in a concrete situation (Knox, 1982). In a highly complicated world, planners can only strive to make the best judgments. Planning practice is rarely a matter of knowing unambiguously what is right; it is more a process of choosing from among competing alternatives. Good planning, then, is a matter of making the most defensible judgments about what to do in light of what is possible (as defined by the constraints imposed by circumstances) and what is desirable (as defined by a set of values and beliefs). If what planners do is make judgments, it follows that better planning will result from knowing more about the process by which these judgments are made. The process by which planning problems are solved, which has been called *deliberation* (Schwab, 1969) and *practical reasoning* (Reid, 1979), consists of formulating decision points, devising alternative choices at these points, considering arguments for and against various alternatives, and choosing the most defensible alternative based on what is possible and desirable (Walker, 1971). In this view, educators of adults become expert planners by developing and being aware of their own criteria for making decisions and knowing how the criteria are to be used in concrete situations. Rather than applying standard principles, the naturalistic viewpoint places primary emphasis on the planner's ability to make judgments in a specific context and to justify them.

The most elegant and well-articulated example of this viewpoint in adult education is Houle's two-part system of program design (1972). The system's first part establishes a series of seven choices, "each of which requires both an analysis of a complex situation and a selection among alternative courses of action" (Houle, 1972, p. 223). He clearly points out that the decision points are not a logical series of steps (the practical world is much too complicated for that) but a complex of interacting elements that are dealt with at various points throughout the planning process. Because Houle believes that planners' choices are strongly influenced by the context in which they are made, the second part of his system requires the planner to determine in which of eleven categories of educational design situations (for example, individuals design their own activities, teachers design an activity for a group) the proposed learning activity belongs. In a more recent incarnation of the naturalistic viewpoint, Brookfield (1986) urges program planners to recognize that they are "practical theorists" who must use their intuition to make judgments about what to do in specific contexts, a task for which "the neatly conceived models of practice found in manuals and textbooks" (p. 245) are inadequate. In planning programs, practical theorists are exquisitely sensitive to the context and base their judgments of what to do on their own values and on theories of action about what works in the real world. As Knox (1982) explains about the decision-making process, "Although choosing among alternative courses of action seems to be the focus, the process includes attention to the context in which decisions are made and implemented, mastery of technical procedures, interpersonal relations, consideration of both individual and organizational values, and concepts about organization and administration" (p. 8).

By providing the conceptual tools for understanding the two major determinants of good planning, that is, *making decisions* in a *specific context,* the theorists for this viewpoint hope to improve educators' abilities to make the best judgments in practice. This expresses the central characteristic of the naturalistic viewpoint: planning systems do not make choices in the real world, planners do. Because education is a practical art, program planners are judged by how well they deal with concrete planning situations in which they have a specific group of learners (not the generic adult learner), a specific organizational context, and limited resources of money and time. In this regard, Knox (1982) has stressed the situation-specific nature of planning and thus the need for practical knowledge. He says that when planners make decisions, they "rely heavily on their intuition, which is based on tacit (or private) knowledge distilled from past experience, common sense, and familiarity with people and the local situation" (p. 13). Thus, as Houle (1972) says, the quality of any particular program "depends in large measure upon the wisdom and competence of the person making the choices" (p. 223).

Although this viewpoint focuses attention on the importance of judgment, context, and values in the program-planning process, the same questions that Tyler asks need to be addressed at some point. Planners still need to ask what the program's purposes will be, what learning experiences will be designed to achieve them, and whether the goals were achieved in the particular setting. For example, Brookfield describes a workshop, "A Critical Look at Creating Staff Development Programs: From Needs Assessment Through Evaluation," that offers to help school administrators devise staff development programs. The major topics he covers include needs assessment, determining objectives and content, determining methods, and evaluation (Brookfield, 1986). Thus, the questions of the classical viewpoint remain important, but the focus is changed to ask how planners answer the questions in a specific practice setting.

By arguing that what planners really do is make judgments through a deliberative process in a specific context, the naturalistic viewpoint offers fresh insights into ways of improving planning practice. It tells its students to look at how real planners justify the choices they make in practice and to learn from the precedents (Dominick, 1990). Despite the value of these insights, questions remain for the planner in practice. Are there any standards, either technical or ethical, for knowing whether a planner has made the "best" judgment? Any choice probably can be justified because the naturalistic viewpoint does not prescribe the values or precedents on which planners *should* base their judgments. Furthermore, this process of deliberation, or practical reasoning, appears to be too rational, for it does not address the situations in which unequal relationships of power exist between the educator and others involved in the planning process. Nor does it address those everyday situations in which rational processes of deliberation are impractical. It does, however, begin to highlight the effect of values and ethics on planning and the interpersonal nature of planning.

The essential idea we take from the naturalistic viewpoint for our own planning theory is the importance of examining planning practice. In this view, the distinguishing characteristic of any practice is its action orientation. Even in situations of ambiguity, doubt, or confusion, program planners must decide what needs to be (or not be) said or done. Planners do not have the luxury of eternal doubt, forever wondering which choice to make from a series of alternative courses of action. Sometimes the choices appear to be easy, and at other times planners must choose from among equally attractive (any one of the potential instructors is acceptable) or unattractive (whatever content is selected for the program, someone will be left out) alternatives. Most often, planning practice is embedded in the complicated organizational world in which problems are not well formed and unambiguous but messy and indeterminate. As Reid (1979) says, "Problems are uncertain when the grounds for decision-making are unclear, when there are conflicting aims, when the problems relate to unique contexts, and when other people with varying wants and desires are affected by solutions to them" (p. 195). In this view, the judgments that planners make are practical, because the problems they face are fundamentally uncertain; that is, they require judgments about what to do and are characteristically ambiguous. In this view, practical judgments have as much to do with what problem needs to be solved as with how to solve it.

The Critical Viewpoint

Planners can make the best judgments in everyday practice, the theories of the critical viewpoint argue, only if they clearly understand that education is a political and ideological activity intimately connected with the social inequalities of society as a whole. Because the judgments are made in a world of unequal and shifting relationships of power, they are inherently ethical and political, not technical. Therefore, all educators operate from an identifiable set of interests that drive and shape their planning activities (Carr and Kemmis, 1986; Habermas, 1971). Thus, by identifying their interests, planners have a clear standard by which to make these judgments if they are to play a progressive role in creating a more equal and humane society. Educators must always have an interest in emancipation that is guided by the values of "equity, sharing, personal dignity, security, freedom, and caring" (Beyer and Apple, 1988, p. 7). The concern for social and political emancipation marks this viewpoint. Unlike the theories of the other two viewpoints, the critical viewpoint claims to have a set of explicit moral standards by which program planners abide so that a planner "openly takes sides in the interest of struggling for a better world" (Giroux, 1983, p. 19). Much of the theorizing of the critical viewpoint has sought to uncover how schools serve society's dominant political, cultural, and economic interests at the expense of those not in these groups (Apple, 1982, 1990; Beyer and Apple, 1988; Giroux, 1983). The goal of curriculum theory, then, is to show the way toward a reconstruction of society's cultural, political, and economic relations through education and schooling. The theorists have developed a "critical pedagogy" to challenge the hegemony of existing relationships of power, which can guide educators involved in "counterhegemonic" practice.

Drawing from the work of critical curriculum theorists (see Pinar and Bowers, 1992, for a comprehensive review), a stream of theories in adult education is emerging that accounts for the central role played in the planning process by interpersonal, organizational, and societal relationships of power and proposes a clear ethical standard to guide planners in creating a more equal society (Freire, 1970; Griffin, 1983; Hart, 1990; Shor and Freire, 1987). Although the tradition of adult educators working in the interests of radical social reform (Cunningham, 1989) is long-standing, only recently have their insights and motivations become a legitimate basis for planning theory. Clearly, Freire's work in developing a critical pedagogy, or a *Pedagogy of the Oppressed,* has been a guiding beacon for all theorists of the critical viewpoint. He proposes a program-planning practice that liberates people by helping them find their voice, which has been suppressed by existing structures that promote social inequality. In a similar vein, Hart (1990) discusses the principles of developing programs for consciousness raising, which include "the actual experience of power on the individual level, a theoretical grasp of power as a larger social reality, and a practical orientation toward emancipatory action" (p. 71). Where, for example, Freire has developed a planning theory that accounts for his work with illiterate men and women in Brazil and Hart has developed a set of principles for consciousness-raising groups, others (Griffin, 1983; Welton, 1987) have argued for more comprehensive theories. Griffin (1983) calls for a general "curriculum theory of adult and lifelong education . . . which is addressed to the problems of the aims, content, and methods of adult learning in a context of knowledge, culture, and power" (p. 200). Although he believes that Freire and others raise the important issues that any

planning theory must address, such as whether adult education reproduces or transforms existing social and political inequalities,
these issues have not been incorporated into any general program-
planning theory.

The writers who adhere to the critical viewpoint have self-
consciously focused on the development of theory to account for the
political and ethical issues central to education. They do not apol-
ogize for this emphasis on theory, because "how to" questions can
only be dealt with after "why" questions have been explored and
provisionally resolved (Beyer and Apple, 1988). In fact, those sympathetic to the critical viewpoint are struggling to find ways to
fashion practices that are informed by the theory: "the central project I see for critical pedagogues now is actualizing what individuals
like Giroux have theorized" (Tierney, 1990, p. 391). This has led to
vigorous debate regarding what critical pedagogy looks like and
what its effects are in actual practice. Forester (1993) makes a similar
point, saying that the attempt to apply the insights of the critical
viewpoint to planning is in its early stages. In particular, he explains that "Habermas's work . . . provides a framework rather than
a series of particular explanations. It brings us insistently to the
intersection of concerns with action, rationality, politics, structural
change, and history—and then leaves us to carry out more concrete
analyses" (p. 13).

The critical viewpoint, however, has been criticized on several
important counts. Ellsworth's attempt (1989) to plan a university
course, "Media and Anti-Racist Pedagogies," incorporating the interests of emancipation and social justice identifies some central cri-
tiques of this viewpoint. She claims that most theorists who invoke
the central concepts of critical pedagogy (such as individual freedom,
social justice, and social change) rarely locate their discussions
within actual practices that a curriculum planner might use. While
these concepts may be appropriate for the philosophical discussion
of universal values (democracy and justice), this curriculum theory
provides only the most abstract, decontextualized criteria for "thinking through and planning classroom practices to support the
political agenda" (Ellsworth, 1989, p. 300) of the course. Thus,
Ellsworth concludes that educators really do not know what
planners are supposed to do in actual practice. Even more damaging,

perhaps, is Ellsworth's critique of the effects of this approach to curriculum planning, namely that there is no empirical evidence to suggest that this approach actually alters the cultural, economic, or political relationships of power, either inside or outside schools. In fact, based on her own research in planning the course, she concludes that the central concepts of critical pedagogy (empowerment, student voice, dialogue, and even the term *critical*) are repressive myths that maintain relationships of domination in the classroom. When the participants in the class tried to put into practice the theoretical prescriptions for the concepts, "we produced results that were not only not helpful, but actually exacerbated the very conditions we were trying to work against, including Eurocentrism, racism, sexism, classism, and 'banking education' " (Ellsworth, 1989, p. 298). The participants thus had to move away from the theory's myths about what should happen and into classroom practices with specific contexts in order to reach their goals.

The theories of the critical viewpoint draw attention to the political and ethical nature of program planning. The insights they provide show how existing organizational and societal relationships of power shape planners' everyday judgments and encourage them to plan in ways that foster dialogue, democracy, individual freedom, and social justice. Yet this viewpoint falls short in exploring the ways these insights might be worked out in the everyday world faced by program planners. As one of the major theorists of the critical viewpoint points out, "We have a relatively highly developed body of meta-theory, but a seriously underdeveloped tradition of applied, middle-range work" (Apple, 1986, p. 200). It is especially difficult to envision how program planners might practice this viewpoint in organizations that are not committed to the particular political and ethical agenda espoused in the theories, a common situation for many educators of adults. For example, how are educators who are personally committed to these goals to plan programs in the face of an organizational mandate to make a profit? Surely, the theories of this viewpoint ought to suggest some way to help these program planners.

The essential idea that we take from the critical viewpoint for our own planning viewpoint is that planning practice is inherently a social, political, and ethical activity. Planners' basic work does involve deliberation and practical judgments (as assumed by the naturalistic viewpoint). What is missing from that viewpoint is provided here—namely, that program planners make judgments based on personal, institutional, and social interests. Practice is inextricably connected to institutional contexts that have a history, are composed of interpersonal and organizational relationships of power, and are marked by conflicting wants and interests. Thus, planners make judgments about what to say and do in situations that are intensely influenced by organizational politics, historical precedents, and the conflicting intentions of all involved in the planning. Planners' practical judgments are social, not only with regard to envisioning feasible and desirable alternative courses of action in their *specific* organizational context but also with regard to negotiating with others, choosing among conflicting wants and interests, developing trust, locating support and opposition, being sensitive to timing, and knowing the informal ropes as well as the formal organizational chart (Forester, 1989).

The classical viewpoint is an abstract model of an ideal system of planning but does not help educators understand everyday practice or action. After all, according to the naturalistic viewpoint, planners are real people who have to decide what action to take in the real world. For a planning theory to be genuinely helpful, then, it must account for how planners actually deliberate. This view forcefully draws attention to the practical contexts of action and the process by which planners make planning judgments in those contexts. But what about the personal, institutional, and social interests (and the concomitant relationships of power) that shape the contexts and therefore the feasibility of planners' judgments? If planners do not take the interests raised by the critical viewpoint into account, they surely will be ineffective. Planning in the face of power and interests is a daily necessity and a constant ethical challenge (Forester, 1989).

Integrating Planners' Discretion
and Structural Constraints

Planners are not free agents, able to choose any course of action they want. Nor, however, are their actions utterly determined by the social and institutional structures in which they work. Although this dichotomy between discretion and structural constraint may be distinguishable in theory, any planning practice must integrate it (Forester, 1989; Goodson, 1991). Yet none of the three planning viewpoints focuses on this necessity. Each emphasizes one element or the other of the dichotomy. The classical viewpoint assumes that programs emerge from the application of a set of prescribed planning steps: answer some permutation of Tyler's four questions in any planning situation, and a program will emerge. This viewpoint privileges planners' discretion at the expense of structural constraint; it offers no perspective on how the context affects planning. Such extreme individualism unrealistically empowers individuals with an unconstrained ability to act meaningfully in the world, because the theories make a strong, and ultimately untenable, set of assumptions about planning. This view of planning, which Forester (1989) terms *comprehensive rationality* assumes that the planner has a well-defined problem to solve, a full array of alternatives, complete information about the context and the consequences of each alternative, and unlimited time, skill, resources. Of course, the problem with these assumptions is that they have to be radically altered in real planning situations.

The naturalistic viewpoint compensates for this overly idealistic sense of reality by arguing that planners' actions are fundamentally "bounded" by the constraints of a situation. In contrast to the classical viewpoint, the naturalistic models assume that the planner is working with ill-defined problems to solve, incomplete information about the alternatives and their consequences, and limited time, skill, and resources (Forester, 1989). This viewpoint focuses planning practice on the relationships among people in their discussions, deliberations, and arguments about what to do (Barone, 1988; Egan, 1988; Posner, 1988). Like the classical viewpoint, however, it also tends to privilege discretion at the expense of structural constraint, for it makes deliberation the province of individual planners (Walker, 1975). While it somewhat illuminates the direct bearing of context on planners' actions, the naturalistic viewpoint does not provide clear insights into the dynamics of conflicts or into the contexts in which they occur. Although the naturalistic viewpoint, in contrast to the classical viewpoint, recognizes that programs evolve within a context and are severely constrained by its demands, it still sees planning practice and action as primarily within the discretion of planners.

The critical viewpoint weighs in on the other side of the dichotomy by proposing that educational programs are largely determined by structural forces, namely the dominant ideologies and interests of social, cultural, and political institutions. In this perspective, the interests of social and institutional organizations transcend, and ultimately minimize, planners' discretion. In other words, structure is privileged at the expense of individual choice. Yet this viewpoint offers important contributions to the understanding of planning practice. Rather than focusing on planners' individual discretion, it stipulates that planners must clearly understand that the interests embedded in the institutional context inevitably determine what planners do and what they must do.

Although these three viewpoints offer important insights into planning practice, they are necessarily incomplete because people cannot act in the real world as the theories assume. In other words, they are based on flawed versions of human action (Bernstein, 1971; Bernstein, 1983; Hawkesworth, 1989; Lave, 1988). Planners always act within a context and as Forester (1989) has argued so well, ignoring the demands of the context is like walking across an intersection with your eyes closed. This is a powerful image because it offers a useful metaphor for integrating planners' discretion and structural constraint. Like planning, crossing a heavily traveled street is a practical, not a theoretical, activity. Both require an integration of human discretion within the constraints that fundamentally structure the activity. Street crossers have to take notice of the behavior of other people acting within the constraints imposed by traffic. If they do not, they are likely to be run over. Planning practice is much the same: planners must negotiate the interests of other people acting within their organizational structure; otherwise, their programs will fail. Just as the individual crossing the busy intersection must take traffic patterns into account, individuals planning programs in an institutional and social context must recognize that planning is part of *social activity* (Goodson, 1991). The interests embedded in their institutional structures constrain what is possible and desirable so that only a certain range of actions is conceivable. At the same time, planners bring to the planning arena their own interests about what is possible and desirable. For the planner acting in context, programs emerge through the negotiation of multiple interests. The norms of what is possible and desirable are rooted in the organizational settings within which planners act. Consequently, by understanding what interests guide planning practice, educators can understand why programs end up with certain purposes, content, audience, and format.

Model for Planning Practice: Negotiating Interests

We began this chapter by asking what planners do. We believe the essential problem confronting program-planning theory in adult education is that it does not adequately account for the important things that real educators must do in everyday practice (Cervero, 1989; Goodson, 1991). As we argued earlier, we need a view of planning practice that integrates planners' discretion and structural constraint. We see practice as falling within the intellectual traditions that "seek to explain relations between human action and the social or cultural system at the level of everyday activities in culturally organized settings" (Lave, 1988, p. 14). The crucial first step is to move planning out of the minds of individual planners and into the social relations among people working in institutional settings. Thus, planning is essentially a *social* activity in which people negotiate with each other in answering questions about a program's form, including its purposes, content, audience, and format (Goodson, 1991). An educational program is never constructed by a single planner acting outside an institutional and social context. Rather, programs are constructed by people with multiple interests working in specific institutional contexts that profoundly affect their content and form.

Putting practice into its social context inextricably links planners' actions to the complex world of power relationships and interests. As educators construct programs, their actions are structured by the power relationships and interests of all the people who have a stake in the program. These two concepts (power and interests) and their relationship to negotiation are defined and explained in depth in Part Three; we discuss them only briefly here.

Power is the capacity to act, distributed to people by virtue of the enduring social relationships in which they participate (Isaac, 1987). Power is not a specific kind of relationship (such as one of domination) but is rather a necessary characteristic of all relationships among people in the planning process. Power relationships exist in all human interactions and define what people are able to do in a particular planning situation. Thus, planners' actions are structured by the power relationships of their institutional and social contexts.

Interests direct the actions of planners and other people in the planning process and are defined as complex sets of "predispositions embracing goals, values, desires, expectations, and other orientations and inclinations that lead a person to act in one direction or another" (Morgan, 1986, p. 41). In other words, interests are motivations and purposes that lead people to act in certain ways when they must decide what to do or say. Interests are simply the human social purposes that give direction for acting in the world (Carr and Kemmis, 1986; Habermas, 1971). In sum, educational programs are constructed by people with particular interests who have relationships of power with each other.

Power and interests define the social contexts in which planners must act. In order to understand what planners are able to do, their actions must be linked to these contexts. Therefore, to make the connection between planner discretion and structural constraint, we argue that *negotiation* is the central form of action that planners undertake in constructing programs. Negotiation always involves two separate actions that occur simultaneously. First, we draw on the conventional usage of negotiation, which is defined in *Webster's New World Dictionary* (1976) as "to confer, bargain, or discuss with a view to reaching agreement" with others. Within this conventional usage, we employ the obvious meaning that planners always *negotiate with* specific interests and power to construct a program. But we also mean that planners *negotiate between* the interests of other people in any planning process. Planners not only bring their own interests to the planning process (negotiate with), but also deal with the interests of others involved in constructing

the program (negotiate between). This conventional usage of negotiation provides insight into the first important action that planners
undertake, constructing an educational program.

At a more fundamental and encompassing level, planners
also directly *negotiate* the interests and power relationships *themselves*. People's interests and power relationships are not static, but
rather are continually acted on by the negotiation practices themselves. This means that not only do planners negotiate with and
between interests, they also negotiate *about* the interests and power
relationships that structure their planning practice. Planners' actions, while directed toward constructing educational programs, are
also always reconstructing the power relationships and interests of
everyone involved in planning the program. The process of negotiation affects people's interests and power relationships either by
maintaining and strengthening them or by transforming them. We
are thereby arguing that power relationships and interests always
both structure negotiations and are reconstructed by these same
practices. We use this dual sense of negotiation—bargaining between interests and directly affecting interests—to link planners'
actions with the social context of planning. In sum, planners both
act in and act on their settings through negotiation.

By examining actual cases of planning in the next three
chapters, we show how programs are constructed by negotiating
between interests. As these three cases show, neither planners' discretion nor structural constraint alone can account for the forms of
the programs. Each planner is working with a complex array of
interpersonal and institutional interests that ultimately are expressed in the final program. As these three cases illustrate, program
planners must work with situation-specific institutional and human interests that are often in conflict, constantly changing, and
sometimes invisible or at odds with the planners' own values and
intentions. Yet these interests define for planners what is possible,
desirable, and at times, imaginable. Every program will be constructed, then, from the negotiation between these interests within
the social context. Some will rise to prominence, and others will
recede to insignificance in planning an educational program. This
negotiation is expressed in every practical judgment made in creating any educational program, including its purposes, content, au-

dience, and format. Every aspect of a program represents the interests that were part of its creation. Responsible planning practice requires an active awareness of the multiple interests within the social context.

How does a program come to be? Its ultimate form, both as represented in the abstract in a brochure or syllabus and as experienced by participants, emerges from the everyday activities of those who planned it. Programs are fashioned through the planning practices of many people in the concrete settings of institutional life. In our view, questions about a prospective program's purposes, content, audience, and format are important, but they are not givens to work with or toward. Rather, they are practical and political problems to be formulated and continually reconstructed through daily practice (Forester, 1989). How program planners negotiate interests to answer these questions is the central problem of their practice.

This model of planning as a social activity in which planners negotiate interests can improve practice in three ways. First, it makes sense of much of the apparent noise of daily work. Negotiations are conducted through the daily informal conversations, public planning meetings, countless telephone calls, memoranda, letters, and faxes now endemic in the modern organization. A model that moves planning out of the minds of planners and into the social relations among people accounts for the everyday activities of planning practice. Second, this model inescapably identifies planning as a political activity. It is simply impossible to plan an educational program without attending to the interests of the institution or its relationships of power. Negotiating between these interests, along with those of the planner, the potential learners, those teaching in the program, and the affected public, is fundamentally a political act. Some interests will become central to the planning of a program, while others will be downplayed. In those instances where consensus reigns among all interested parties regarding the purposes, content, audience, and format of a program, the negotiation will appear to proceed easily. However, this should not mask the fact that negotiation is occurring. Much more often, there will be uncertainties, ambiguities, and conflict that must be resolved in planning a program.

Finally, this model more clearly defines the ethical responsibilities of planners. Because planners are no longer regarded as neutral actors, the central ethical question here is whose interests will be represented by which people in constructing the educational program. This is more difficult because it is not a judgment made once and for all at the beginning of the planning; rather, interests are continually being negotiated throughout all the activities that form a specific program. In the messy world of organizational politics, it is often easiest to do what works. However, program planners frequently feel at odds with the dominant organizational interest. This can happen, for example, when the organizational interest of making a profit from a program by enrolling large numbers of participants creates an educational format that effectively silences participants. This model alone does not offer ethical standards that can be applied in every situation. In Part Three, we take up the question of what ethical standards should guide educators' practices in planning programs for adults. However, by drawing attention to the centrality of interests to planning, this model can identify the important types of judgments planners routinely make in shaping every educational program.

$$=== \quad PART\ 2 \quad ===$$

Negotiating Interests
in Planning Practice:
Three Cases

At the end of Chapter Two, we introduced the model of negotiating interests as the central activity of planning. Part Two shows how this model can make sense of planners' work; it provides an account of how three educational programs were actually constructed. The cases are central to the book because we believe that any attempt to understand practice has to be fundamentally grounded in what program planners actually do. In order to develop a rich account of practice, we sought planners who worked in different types of organizations and whose programs served different educational purposes. We selected the three cases because they offer recognizable examples of program-planning situations in adult education. Each chapter is organized in the same way. The two opening sections introduce the primary planners and their organizational settings and provide a calendar of the major events and meetings that occurred during planning. The third section describes the major interests the planners negotiated in constructing the program. In the final section, we show how these interests directly shaped people's judgments about the purposes, audience, content, and format for each program. Although we use fictitious names for the organizations and the planners, all other information in the chapters is real. We have also modified the documents that appear as exhibits, but the information contained in each exhibit is accurate.

In Chapter Three, we describe how the primary planners, Pete and Joan, plan a management education program at the Phoenix Company. The central interest in this case was to fix an organizational problem, the breakdown in communication throughout the company. We also describe how Pete and Joan represented two other interests in planning this program: to change the basis of the company's management education programs from didactic to more experiential and to strengthen the power of the human resources department within the company.

In Chapter Four, we examine a market-driven continuing education program being developed within State University's College of Pharmacy. Although the primary interest in this program, as represented by Carl, Bob, and Richard, was to maintain the leadership of the college in the profession through continuing education, we describe the importance of economic and regulatory interests in constructing the program.

Chapter Five introduces Marti, a program coordinator in the Organization for Persons with Disabilities, who is planning a program to help employers understand and implement the provisions of the Americans with Disabilities Act. Marti and Ann, director of the organization, negotiate the social advocacy interest of improving the lives of people with disabilities. In addition, the chapter shows how the other interests—to produce funds to support other programs in the organization and to enhance the image of the organization—were also crucial to understanding how the program was constructed. Unlike the other two programs, this one was canceled because of insufficient enrollment. However, the cases are not presented for the purpose of comparing programs that "succeeded" and one that "failed"; rather, they are presented to illustrate the ways in which the negotiation model makes sense of everyday planning practice. Chapter Five also makes evident how Marti's planning practices furthered the interests of the organization, regardless of whether the program was held.

THREE

Fixing an Organization Through Management Education

The Phoenix Company is a service-oriented business with 1,280 employees in the southeastern United States. The company had conducted an annual management retreat for ten years, which was planned by the president, to inform department directors of the plans of the company for the upcoming year. Because he was vice president for human resources, Pete was one of the primary planners for the 1992 annual retreat. The other primary planner for this retreat was Joan, whom Pete had recently hired as the company's director of customer service. Pete and Joan had an interest in changing the purpose and format of the retreat. They transformed the retreat from an activity in which vice presidents provided information about their plans for the upcoming year into a management education program designed to remedy an organizational problem. The problem, as defined by top management, was that the processes for communicating information throughout the company were not working well.

As Exhibit 3.1 shows, the program planning took approximately four months. This included three initial meetings with the company president, Sam Jones, during January and February 1992. During the third meeting, Pete and Joan received approval to hire George (the director of a leadership center at a nearby university) as a consultant to facilitate the program. Pete, Joan, and George had three planning meetings during March and April. The retreat

Exhibit 3.1. Program Planning Calendar.

September 21–22, 1990	Most recent company management retreat.
September 1, 1991	Joan hired as director of customer service.
January 2, 1992	Pete and Joan have first meeting about the upcoming retreat with Sam Jones, the company president.
January 17, 1992	Second meeting with the president.
February 13, 1992	Third meeting with the president.
February 21, 1992	Pete and Joan send memorandum to audience announcing retreat purpose and dates.
March 6, 1992	Pete and Joan have first meeting to plan the retreat with George, an outside consultant hired to facilitate retreat.
March 20, 1992	Second meeting with George.
April 9, 1992	Pete and Joan send memorandum to audience with final retreat schedule.
April 27, 1992	Third meeting with George.
May 7–8, 1992	Phoenix Company Management Retreat.

was held at a conference site sixty miles from the company in early May 1992.

History and Institutional Setting

The company has a president, five vice presidents, and thirty-eight department heads. Figure 3.1 shows the company's formal organizational chart. Pete reports to the president through the executive vice president, although all vice presidents sit on the company's policy management team and comprise the top management team. Joan is one of five department heads who report directly to Pete. The company's middle management has two levels: the thirty-eight department heads and the sixty-five line supervisors. However, twenty supervisors who report to the department heads in the professional services division of the company have technical training and responsibility for the company's core product. As a result, these twenty people have a level of authority and degree of control similar to the department heads, although their positions were not at that level in the formal organizational chart. All previous management retreats included the president, the six vice presidents, and all thirty-

Figure 3.1. Phoenix Company Organizational Chart.

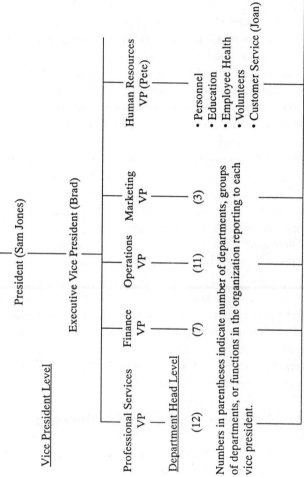

Board of Directors

President (Sam Jones)

Executive Vice President (Brad)

Vice President Level

| Professional Services VP | Finance VP | Operations VP | Marketing VP | Human Resources VP (Pete) |

Department Head Level

(12)   (7)   (11)   (3)

- Personnel
- Education
- Employee Health
- Volunteers
- Customer Service (Joan)

Numbers in parentheses indicate number of departments, groups of departments, or functions in the organization reporting to each vice president.

Line Supervisor Level (65 reporting to the 38 department heads) Each department head has 1 to 8 supervisors.

eight department heads. The 1992 program had a significantly larger and different audience because it included for the first time the twenty technical supervisors as well as all the new department heads who had been appointed in the usual course of employee turnover.

Pete, a cheerful and gregarious individual who considers himself a "humanist," had worked at the company for ten years. As vice president, a position he has held for six years, he is responsible for a number of functions in the company, including customer service, public relations, personnel, employee health, and education. Joan worked at the company for several years as the director of customer service. She left the company in March 1990 for a position at another firm. She remained at the new firm until September 1991 when she was rehired for her old job at the Phoenix Company. Pete was pleased to have Joan back, because the woman he had hired to replace her had left after twelve months, having been rebuffed by the president and executive vice president in her attempt to change the organizational culture.

Pete and Joan have a great deal of respect for one another and, having worked together for several years, have a relationship with which both feel comfortable and in which they believe they complement each other. For example, in describing how they planned for a recent meeting with the company president, Joan says, "We'll sit and we'll talk [about what to do because] Pete and I are real idea people, and we bounce things off each other." Then she prepares the meeting agenda because "he likes it done, but I'm the one who does it. That's just my personality. We've worked together long enough. He knows that's the way I am, and that's ok." Pete echoes this interpretation of their relationship in describing how they prepared an agenda for another meeting with the president: "I asked Joan to write it up for us, but we mutually talked about what to put on it [the agenda], and Joan put it down on paper for us." Both planners wanted to change the retreat so that it served an educational rather than an informational function. Joan considers herself a "driver personality" who becomes impatient with how long it takes to change the way her organization operates. Although Pete too is deeply committed to changing the organization, he expects it will take time. "If adults become aware of some deficiencies and problems, then many times they're willing to try to change them," Pete said. "And if we give them the right tools and the right encouragement, many times they're successful in doing so. I don't think we can dictate or manipulate behavior too much. But if people see the need and know that's what we're expecting, then sometimes a light comes on."

Pete has a fair amount of latitude in planning the overall management education program. His department offers many programs for all levels of company management during the year; many are based on suggestions or requests from the target audience. For example, his department conducts surveys and telephone polls to get "input from people and be responsive and at the same time move our needs along," he said. Moving along the company's needs (as defined by top management) takes top priority, as Pete explains. "If we [top management] think it's important, then they [participants] think it's important. We are pretty directive in our approach to planning things," Pete said. "I guess I'm pretty directive because I see myself as kind of the internal OD [organizational development] person who has my finger on what's happening . . . and I feel pretty strongly that my ideas are valid and felt by the managers."

Pete and Joan were the primary planners of the management education program discussed in this chapter. The annual spring retreats at the company have been a "real sacred cow," Pete said. The company president, Jones, has planned them as an opportunity for each vice president to outline plans and policies for the coming year: Pete said, "It was very directive and everybody rotated to each VP and were told this is what we're doing and here's our budget plans and then you went home." One year the retreat would be held in town and the next year out of town. However, there was no history of using the annual retreat for educational purposes until the most recent one in 1990. That planning process was extremely contentious and provides the background necessary for understanding the planning efforts for the 1992 retreat (no retreat was held in 1991).

In the spring of 1990 (just after Joan had left the company), Pete had wanted to develop a retreat program that was more of a "communication, interaction kind of thing but Mr. Jones was not ready to do it at all . . . he said that he might want to do it in the fall but I never heard from him again" until he [Pete] was confronted by Brad, the executive vice president, Pete said. As Pete described it,

> We [Pete and Brad] got into a couple of real shouting matches in the budget preparation that I didn't understand why, but apparently the executive VP believed I was trying to undermine his authority and that I was questioning his judgment in an inappropriate way. He really got upset about it. So then, in the summer of 1990, we continued to have disagreements, and that's when he shook his finger in my face one day in July and said, "Goddammit, where is our retreat, Pete? The boss said he wants to have a retreat; I just talked to him last night, and he wonders why you haven't planned it, and his understanding was that you were going to do one in August and why haven't you got this together?" That's exactly what he said in front of a whole group of people when I had not even heard the word *retreat* in the last sixty days. Much less had been given the mandate to do it.

So Pete pulled together a retreat using Harvard Business School cases as directed by Brad, secured the site, and hired an outside consultant from a nearby university to facilitate the session. In Pete's view, the program "ended up being a real success, very positive." The outcome of this retreat was a pivotal point in Pete's role in the organization. By fall 1991, Pete saw himself as the point person in moving along the organizational change: "I feel I've been given permission and authority to be the organizational culture person and to push things. So I feel as though they depend on me. I feel as though I've got the leadership role there." He was also feeling much more confident about his place in the organization than he had while planning the previous retreat. "I'm in a much different position in the organization as far as the politics of this management team," he said, "because, you see, the last time I was a sinking ship going into this thing and this time I'm on top of things." The company skipped the 1991 annual retreat because, according to Pete, the timing was not right. So the group of vice presidents had not gotten together in a retreat (or any other educational program) for more than a year when Joan was rehired in September 1991. Then, Pete and Joan began to identify organizational problems that needed to be addressed through management education.

The Program: Phoenix Company Management Retreat

The retreat was held on a Thursday and Friday during the first week in May at a resort sixty miles from the company. Of the sixty-five people invited, sixty-two were present. They arrived late Thursday morning for the lunch that opened the retreat. The program ended at 1:30 Friday afternoon. Exhibit 3.2 shows the retreat schedule much as it was distributed at the opening session. Thursday was primarily devoted to team-building exercises set up by an outside consulting firm, Executive Adventures. This firm conducts outdoor activities emphasizing physical interaction in order to strengthen interpersonal relationships. The planners contracted for this packaged program, and neither they nor George had any role as facilitators; they participted along with all company employees. These exercises were conducted in groups of thirteen that had been selected in advance by Pete and Joan. The Executive Adventures firm was not involved in planning the Friday sessions. Thursday evening, dinner was held at the inn with social activities organized by Pete and Joan. Each of the three separate activities scheduled for Friday morning was designed to facilitate the achievement of the stated retreat objectives. All three activities used both small and large groups. In the workshop entitled "Departmental Meetings—Disaster or Success?" George asked the small groups to identify characteristics of successful and unsuccessful meetings to give the participants ideas about how to conduct effective meetings. In the "Desert Survival Exercise," small groups simulated being lost in the wilderness and tried to save themselves. In the large group discussion after this, George helped people to see different ways that they "saved themselves," which stresses the importance of communicating as a team member. For the "Departmental Meetings Exercise," Pete wrote three role-playing scenarios based on actual

Exhibit 3.2. Phoenix Company Management Retreat Agenda.

Retreat Objectives

1. To increase the awareness of the importance to the Phoenix Company of communicating as a team member. This includes but is not limited to supporting others, leading in a positive manner, working cooperatively with other departments, projecting a positive image about the department and Phoenix Company, and resolving problems in a quiet, positive manner for the good of the company.
2. To provide skill-building opportunities on "How to Conduct a Meeting."
3. To provide opportunities to develop skills in handling difficult questions, conflict, and confrontation when conducting a meeting.

Thursday, May 7, 1992

12:00–1:00 P.M.	Lunch at retreat site
1:00–1:15 P.M.	Welcome, overview and purpose of retreat..............................Pete
1:15–5:15	Executive Adventure Exercises
5:00–7:00	Free time
7:00 until	Outdoor barbecue and social time

Friday, May 8, 1992

7:00–8:00	Breakfast buffet
8:30–8:40	Overview and purpose of morning activities............................Pete
8:45–10:00	Departmental Meetings—Disaster or Success?........................George
10:00–10:15	Break
10:15–11:15	Desert Survival Exercise............George
11:15–12:15	Departmental Meetings Exercise....Pete and George
12:15–1:15	Lunch
1:15–1:30	Summary and wrap-up...............Joan
	Closing comments..............Sam Jones

---

problems that the company was facing, such as the implementation of a new smoking policy for employees. The role playing, which was intended to help participants learn to deal with difficult questions when conducting a meeting, was enacted in small groups. George facilitated the large group discussion that sought to draw lessons from the role playing.

Interests and the Phoenix
Company Management Retreat

This section returns to September 1991 and shows how Pete and Joan's planning practices constructed the Phoenix Company Management Retreat. Pete and Joan continually negotiated about three critically important interests in planning the educational program. The primary interest was to improve the way that the management of the company communicates with the rest of the company's employees (approximately twelve hundred people). This interest was shared by all the significant planners, while the other two interests were shared primarily by Pete and Joan. Pete and Joan wanted to change the approach of management education in the company to a more problem-based and experiential mode and to strengthen support for the company's human resource function.

Improving Organizational Communication

There was widespread agreement among top management that the processes of communicating information throughout the company were not working well. This problem was causing conflict and was so disruptive that the work of the company was not as effective and efficient as it needed to be. Therefore, top management had an interest in improving the organizational communication practices so that decisions were clearly communicated by middle management to all company employees, and middle management was capable of dealing effectively with potential or actual problems at a local level, preventing them from blowing up and disrupting the entire company. The president's interest clearly was to prevent the disruptions that had been occurring because his management team did not communicate effectively with company employees. Pete explained that Jones "has this monthly meeting with hourly employees, and they keep telling him over and over again that we don't know what's going on, our supervisor doesn't answer our questions. They criticize other departments in a department meeting, and they never get any follow-up." The president believed that lack of effective communication had been an ongoing problem at the company.

As Joan noted, when she was interviewing for her position, Jones "talked with me about the need to have better communication from department level up and down." The president's interest, then, was not in changing the organizational relationships of power between management and staff but in fixing the current system so that it would run more smoothly.

Based on the problems they had observed and experienced over the past several years, Pete and Joan shared the desire of other members of top management to minimize staff disputes and conflict and more effectively communicate the directives of the formal leaders of the company. Pete explained this to George in the March 6 planning meeting. "For their manager never to sit down and communicate, that to me means we're missing something," Pete said. From this view, if the company were to function smoothly, department heads would need to communicate the decisions of top management. Department managers not only had to communicate these decisions to company employees but had to do so in a way that would make employees feel they are part of the company "team"; employees needed an opportunity to ask questions and voice complaints. This view of communication did not mean that employees were being given a role in making the decisions. Rather, management needed to communicate better with them so that employees could further the agenda of the company. Pete was clear about this desire to have a particular form of communication and teamwork. During the March 6 planning meeting, he explained his view to George: "How do you conduct a meeting with thirty hourly employees so that you give clear information? You allow for questions and challenges and complaints. But you then keep a teamwork spirit; you keep a positive representation of the company as you respond and not criticize top management."

Pete also had a personal interest in improving the communication skills of the managers. For example, he noted that:

> I'm the person that hears all the grievances, and I'm the person who goes to federal court when we get a lawsuit for terminating someone. So I have a real applicable and valuable reason for wanting managers to be good communicators. I find also that by the time

I'm called in to resolve a problem in a department, it's usually some confrontation, some resistance to communication that's been building for months. And I was just eaten up and spit out for lunch recently in a two-and-a-half hour meeting with a group of twenty employees who were just so angry that they weren't being heard in their department meetings.

In his role as human resource vice president, Pete personally dealt with problems that occurred when middle managers did not communicate effectively with employees. He was left to clean up the messes "that should have been taken care of a little bit at a time over the last three or four months," he said. Thus, Pete's personal and organizational interests converge in wanting to improve communication practices at the company.

Reorienting Management Education

For several years before the 1992 program, Pete had had a clear interest in changing management education from an information-oriented didactic format to a more problem-based experiential approach. He believed that management education was not improving the Phoenix Company. Although Pete represented this interest, it was generally not shared by other members of top management or by the president. Pete had tried to change the orientation of the 1990 retreat by introducing the "concept of executive adventure and focus[ing] on team building, communication with employees, but that was not an option. They would not approve that," Pete recalled. There had been simply no support among the top management team for reorienting management education. Since then, however, Pete had been actively promoting the new orientation to management education in his other planning efforts by, for instance, having department directors "facilitate management training programs . . . when we have not done much of that before." Pete was moving his department toward focusing more on the company's problems as a basis for education, which required the use of internal "facilitators" because "they're usually more in tune with what our needs are than someone from the university," Pete said.

"But they know where we are and are usually real familiar with the terms." In the interview Joan conducted before hiring George, she explained their orientation for the upcoming retreat in these same terms. The focus of the retreat this time was to change the managers' awareness or behavior "by doing group activities versus lecturing about how to be a good manager. Let's look at practicing it," Joan said. Pete and Joan's interest in reorienting management education was evolving and showing up in many of their recent program-planning efforts.

Strengthening the Human Resource Function

Historically, the human resource department of the Phoenix Company had relatively less power than the other functions, such as finance, professional services, and operations, represented by the team of vice presidents. One of Pete's major interests was to secure the power necessary to influence the direction of the company within the top management team. Pete's near powerlessness was demonstrated by the problems he encountered in planning the 1990 retreat. Since then, he had begun to solidify support for the human resource function. Still, he was not fully secure as he began planning for the 1992 retreat. In going into the January 2 meeting with Jones, he was less concerned about obtaining approval for the retreat than about protecting himself from the president's "coming up at the last minute and saying, 'Where's the retreat?'" as had happened in planning the 1990 retreat. Pete was in a continual battle to secure support and power for his role from the president and other members of the top management team. His planning strategy for this retreat was a direct expression of his interest in strengthening his role within the company. Pete decided that he would not include the executive vice president, Brad, at all in planning the 1992 program but that "I was going to make sure that Mr. Jones was part of every step. And so I intentionally excluded Brad because I did not want his input. But I had the power and support to get around him." However, Pete knew that he needed approval for this new approach from other key vice presidents. He had learned from the last retreat that "there are some political players in the vice president team, that it is good to go and run ideas by them and warm them up to what's going on. So I went by and talked to three vice presidents about this whole idea." Pete hoped that these planning practices would build more support for his function in the company among the other members of the top management team.

Negotiating About Purposes

The purpose of the retreat was negotiated primarily by Jones, Pete, and Joan, who shared the interest of improving the way that top and middle managers communicated to the rest of the company employees. The overall purpose they negotiated was to improve the managers' communication practices. Although many employees in the company desired better communication from the managers, the important point is that top management's interest defined those communication needs. No other interests, such as those of the middle managers or the other twelve hundred company employees, were considered in the negotiations. Thus, top management's definition of the communication needs of the company determined the fundamental purpose of the program. While the program's purpose was discussed, Pete and Joan experienced little conflict because no potentially competing interests were involved.

The first, and most important, part of their strategy was to clearly define who was going to be a player in negotiating the purposes. There was no doubt that the president would be the only other significant actor. As Joan said, after she and Pete considered the possibility of using the annual retreat to focus on internal communication, "The first thing we have to do is to talk to Mr. Jones and see what he would like us to do." At their first meeting with the president on January 2, the overall purpose of the program was easily negotiated because all three shared the same interest. Based on this first meeting, Joan felt "We had a good feel for what he wanted accomplished. I think we were all thinking along the same lines." Jones thought it had been long enough since the last retreat and, according to Joan, "gave us the go-ahead" for a spring retreat. At the first meeting, then, the planners successfully negotiated approval to hold the retreat because Jones felt that "communication and having good department meetings were very valid things for us to do," according to Pete. After the program ended, Pete explained that the strategy of representing the president's interests was a crucial aspect of their planning practices. As the final speaker at the Friday lunch, Jones spoke passionately about the importance of the retreat's purpose and, as Pete said, "really tied in the whole communication focus and how employees want to be communicated to." It was unusual that the president was able to do such a good job because "he is not a good speaker and he tends to ramble, but he was just wonderful, he was articulate, he was on the point, he was motivational." Pete reasoned that Jones was able to do this because of his role in negotiating about the purpose of the retreat. "He helped identify the issues in January, we built the whole retreat around issues that were near and dear to him," Pete said. "We were able to brainstorm and get him to identify issues that were also our issues." Thus, the institutional interests of top management were directly expressed in the program.

Pete and Joan were equally clear about who would *not* be involved in negotiating about the program's purpose. In their first planning meeting on March 6, George wanted to know if any other interests were being represented when he asked whether "the people who are coming have bought into the fact that we need some guidance and updating in how to conduct good meetings." Joan's response was, "I don't know." Pete explained after the meeting that it was not that he did not want to seek participation from the managers but that he did not need to because "I feel pretty strongly that my ideas are valid and are felt by managers." In other words, Pete believed that the middle managers shared his ideas about the purpose of the retreat. George pushed the issue of who would negotiate by suggesting that a survey be sent to the audience. Pete said this would be acceptable if the survey would "help warm them up and get some buying in—allow them to participate but not allow them to dictate what we're going to be doing." It was important that top management define the purpose because, as Pete said, "We are running a business."

George's attempts to negotiate about the program's purpose with Pete and Joan offer a second illustration of how they managed to exclude other interests. The fundamental issue was the way in which George interpreted Pete and Joan's interest in improving the communication practices of managers. He saw it as an effort to move the organization to more participatory forms of management. George believed this was a better form of management and assumed that Pete and Joan shared this interest and were trying to reshape the relationships of power at the company. In the negotiation of this issue in the March 6 planning meeting, the fundamental purpose of the retreat became clearer. A question George asked showed that he interpreted the discussion about sending a questionnaire to mean that the purpose of the retreat was to move the company to a more participatory form of management. Pete responded by clearly restating the purpose as defined by top management: "I think the heart of a good meeting, whether you are participatory or not, is in being approachable so that people feel comfortable in raising their hands. And I don't think a lot of times our managers set the climate for people to raise their hand." Pete stopped George's effort to negotiate about the fundamental purpose of the program by reiterating top management's view of effective meetings, namely that employees should feel that their managers are approachable.

In our debriefing after the March 6 meeting, Pete explained that he would not allow George's view to shape the purposes of the program because the managers "would be real threatened by opening the thing up and really talking a lot about participation and participatory decision making. So I kind of sidestepped him, but I think I made it clear to him that we're more directive than we are participatory." This explains why it was so important for Pete to successfully silence George's view. Although Pete was not necessarily opposed to participatory management, he said, "I see us phasing into that and I think we really have to lay a foundation with Mr. Jones to get something like that pulled off." Although George's interest was in moving organizations toward more participatory forms of management, he recognized that Pete was protecting an important organizational interest and did not try to push it.

Negotiating About Audience

The planners made two judgments about the audience that shaped the program. The first was who the members of the audience would be, in other words, who would be invited to attend the retreat.

Second was whether there would be a need to differentiate the roles of top management and middle management at the retreat. This was an issue because the interactive nature of the retreat activities required that all participants be treated equally, although the participants were not equal in the workplace.

Who Should Attend

Historically, the audience for the annual retreat had been the forty-five employees of the company in top management (president and vice presidents) and middle managers (department heads). The issue, as framed up by Pete and Joan for their January 17 meeting with the president, was "whether to have a retreat for all department heads and supervisors (one hundred people) or for just department heads (forty-five people)," Pete said. These forty-five people would include the seven members of top management and the thirty-eight department heads. An intermediate position was to include only those twenty technical supervisors whose authority and degree of control were similar to the department heads'. Thus, the practical judgment facing the planners was how much of middle management should be included and whether the audience should be forty-five, sixty-five, or one hundred people. At their January 17 meeting, Pete, Joan, and Jones decided against "including all supervisory people, but we are including the twenty technically oriented supervisors for the first time," according to Pete.

Two interests shaped Pete and Joan's belief that more people than top management and thirty-eight department heads should be involved. Having more middle managers learn how to communicate better was directly connected to the primary goal of the company in conducting the retreat. If more managers learn how to communicate to employees, they help improve the flow of decisions from top management to the rest of the employees, which should reduce the number of conflicts Pete would have to deal with. In addition, having more managers attend would serve Pete's interest in strengthening support for the human resource function. As Joan explained, "The same forty-five people get all kinds of extra training and benefits, and we never get to the next level." By extending the extra training to the next level of managers, more people would come to see the value of Pete's function in the company. Pete expected the positive assessment to reflect on him because his planning practices made it clear to the other vice presidents that he, and not the president, was pushing this expansion of the audience. Pete discussed this issue with all the vice presidents individually, but most important, "from the professional services vice president, I got a definite green light to include the twenty technically oriented supervisors who report to him," Pete said. Thus, Pete and Joan were prepared for the president's response when they recommended that the twenty supervisors be there. When Jones agreed and asked them to "check with the vice president for professional services," Pete was able to say that professional services had already agreed to include the twenty supervisors.

Pete and Joan recommended limiting the number of supervisors because they felt that "logistically it's real hard and expensive to carry a hundred people out of town overnight and pay for food, lodging, and travel," Pete said. This shows that holding the retreat away from the company was more important to Pete and Joan than including all middle managers.

Roles of the Audience at the Retreat

Pete's interest in reorienting management education at the company forced him to face a fundamental dilemma in negotiating the roles of the audience at the retreat. A well-recognized set of hierarchical relationships of power at the levels of president, vice president, department director, and supervisor governed the workplace. Yet the interactive nature of the retreat during the Executive Adventure and the Friday morning exercises assumed that its members would be treated equally. This had not been a problem at previous retreats in which top management explained their plans for the upcoming year to the department managers; the relationships of power in the workplace had been reproduced at the retreat. Thus, Pete and Joan had to negotiate a transition to a different set of power relationships for the retreat. This negotiation was complicated because Pete and Joan also had to ensure that the temporary equality of roles was not reproduced at the company *after* the retreat. Specifically, the middle managers had to understand that the retreat was not designed to give them more power in the company—the flow of decision making and power would remain the same—but that the goal was to maintain the existing power structure by communicating the decisions of top management better and by running meetings more effectively. Thus, this aspect of negotiating audience roles was tricky because two different interests were involved: the primary interest of improving organizational communication *as defined by top management* and Pete's interest in using an interactive approach to management education that creates a temporary equality among the participants. The potential conflict could have had serious consequences if not resolved in Pete and Joan's planning practices. (The potential conflict was why George thought Pete wanted to promote participatory forms of management.)

The negotiation in regard to the roles of the audience at the retreat is clearest in how the participants for the small group activities were selected. Pete, Joan, and George negotiated in deciding that random assignment was the best way to organize the small groups used for the Executive Adventure and for each activity on Friday morning. In their March 20 meeting, George argued that random assignment to different small groups for all activities would further the primary interest, increasing awareness of the importance of communicating as a team member. Random assignment to four different groups would give people direct experience with most members of the audience. But random assignment of *all* participants to groups led to the problem of how to handle the roles of the president and vice presidents. Pete and Joan were concerned about the president because he typically "pulls his chair out of a group and sits in another part of the room as an observer," Joan said. If this happened at the retreat, it would deal a severe blow to Pete's interest in temporarily renegotiating the power structure for the interactive learning activities. After three planning meetings with the president, they still had no indication that he would participate as an equal although they were hoping and thinking he probably would. They eventually secured his agreement to participate as an active member of the small groups. Because his full and equal participation was so important, it affected their subsequent planning. For example, although all other assignments to small groups were made randomly, the president was placed in Joan's small group for the Executive Adventure. Joan also took the step of explaining to their small group facilitator that "it was real important that we have full participation from him" and that he "not be treated differently."

Pete also needed to negotiate about the roles of the vice presidents during the small group activities. The negotiation occurred during the March 20 planning meeting as Pete, Joan, and George were discussing the desert survival exercise. George explained that the activity would put the small groups in a desert and they would have to decide how to survive the ordeal. When it was over, George would debrief the groups to determine whose ideas were listened to, who took leadership, and whether they used a team approach. Responding to George's description of the activity, Pete said, "We might want to pull out the vice presidents and let them observe . . . I don't know how our VPs will react. I want them involved but I wonder if it might be good for them to be floaters." George responded that he would do just the opposite: "If they do dominate, I'm going to try to process that to discuss who dominated" and analyze that. As George explained, "I would rather have them participate because they are members of the team; otherwise we are having a dichotomy."

Pete explained to us that he went along with including the vice presidents in the activities because it furthered his interest of reorienting management education at the company by fostering temporary equality of power at the retreat. He had suggested pulling the vice presidents out because he was worried that they would "tend to dominate, but then when George said that they would be perceived as monitors" if they did that, Pete realized that would "even be more threatening." Thus, he was comfortable with the judgment, "especially if George explains that everyone is on an equal basis and that no one should dominate the group." This would also further Pete's third interest, to strengthen the support for his function in the company by "getting us closer to confronting the issue that top managers don't feel they have to participate" in the management education programs. By having them participate at the retreat, Pete was hoping the vice presidents would see great value in the human resource function and would participate in future programs.

Negotiating About Content

Pete and Joan negotiated about the content for the retreat with Jones during their January 2 and 17 meetings. The content, which Pete and Joan had written in the language of objectives, expressed the primary interests of improving organizational communication and Pete's interest of reorienting management education at the company. As Pete explained the connection between the 1990 and the 1992 retreats, the objectives were part of a historically developing institutional context: "What we tried to do all along was introduce the concept of executive adventure and focus on team building, communication with employees, and communication among department directors." These interests are clearly evident in the final statement of objectives for the retreat, shown in Exhibit 3.2, which shows both the emphasis on improving organizational communication in objective one and the emphasis on "skill-building opportunities" in conducting meetings in objectives two and three. It is important here to distinguish between the content for the retreat and the *statement* of those objectives in written form. The content for the retreat was decided early in the planning process by Pete, Joan, and Jones and remained constant through the planning. However, the statement of that content went through three versions before the final version was sent in a memorandum to the audience on April 9. Pete allowed George to be involved in negotiating about the statement of objectives because he saw it as a technical activity that would not affect the actual content, which had already been decided.

The first version of objectives for the retreat was prepared by Pete and Joan for their January 17 meeting with Jones. Pete and Joan had based the draft on their January 2 meeting with Jones and on several planning meetings involving only the two of them. The content was stated in the planning document, as shown in Exhibit 3.3. As the first objective shows, this was still early in the planning process, before they had decided whether their audience would include both department heads and supervisors or just department heads. This version shows that even before their second meeting with the president, the primary interest of improving organizational communication (seen in objectives one, three, and four) and

Exhibit 3.3. Retreat Objectives: Original Formulation.

1. To improve department heads' and supervisors' perceptions of how they communicate and how they come across to their staff
2. To give each individual an opportunity to lead a group and to receive feedback on her or his effectiveness
3. To reinforce the value of good communication for managers
4. To provide an opportunity for team building within the management group

Pete's interest of reorienting management education (seen in objective two) had been successfully worked into the content of the program. Pete was even able to explain whose specific interest was represented in each objective: "number one came from Mr. Jones in our January 3 discussion. Number two came more from me because I believe in actually forcing an individual to try it, and three and four came more from Joan's point of view and from the needs we had identified in the fall to reinforce this as a value." Although the statement of objectives would continue to be refined until the April 9 memo was sent, Pete and Joan had by January 17 negotiated about the content with Jones.

The objectives were further refined and a document prepared for Pete and Joan's first meeting with George on March 6. They started the meeting by reviewing the statement of objectives and giving George the rationale for including each one. This list was now beginning to resemble the final one and is shown in Exhibit 3.4. Although the list was simply to be a starting point for their discussion that day, Pete made sure to indicate that some content was not negotiable because of the importance of the interests from which it was constructed. In reference to the first objective, how to conduct a meeting, Pete said, "This comes directly from Mr. Jones, and that information is not getting down to lower levels of the company." In reference to the second objective, Pete explained that the retreat had to give participants actual experiences in handling difficult questions in meetings. "What we're thinking about in doing that is having several exercises" that would simulate a department meeting about a difficult problem, he said. He was conveying to George that his interest in experiential learning was important, that it had to be expressed in the design of the retreat.

Exhibit 3.4. Retreat Objectives: Revised Formulation.

1. To provide skill-building opportunities on "How to Conduct a Meeting."
2. To provide opportunities to develop skills for handling difficult questions, conflict, and confrontation in a meeting.
3. To increase the awareness of the importance to the Phoenix Company of communicating as a team member. This includes but is not limited to supporting others, leading in a positive manner, working cooperatively with other departments, projecting a positive image about the department and Phoenix Company, and resolving problems in a quiet, positive manner for the good of the company.
4. To stress the importance of using positive reinforcement and recognizing people for their good works.

George heard this message and agreed that it was possible to meet all the objectives, even though his immediate reaction was that they might not have enough time; constructing the exercises to meet all the objectives within the time allotted might require further discussion, George said. At the end of the March 6 meeting, George agreed to "review your objectives, maybe putting them in different language," and then meet to determine the final statement of objectives at the March 20 meeting. At that meeting, they agreed to provide more detail about the specific content to be covered, although they already had agreed, as George said, that the "team-building objective [number three] was being met in large measure by the executive adventure. So we're having a segment for each one of the objectives." The list of objectives, as sent to the audience for the retreat, embodied the negotiation about two major interests of top management. Pete and Joan's negotiations with the president had shaped what was to be taught at the program, although the actual statement of the objectives and the specific activities designed to reach the objectives were negotiated with George.

Negotiating About Format

All three interests came into play as Pete and Joan negotiated about the many aspects of the format of the retreat. Of the many judgments the planners made about format, four were critically important in furthering these interests. The first was the *location* at which the retreat was to be held—whether it would be held in the same town as the Phoenix Company or at a remote site. The second concerned the overall *schedule* for the retreat—whether the retreat would be held on Thursday and Friday or Friday and Saturday. The third related to the selection of *instructors* for the retreat; the analysis of this judgment focuses on the selection of the Executive Adventure consulting firm and on why George was hired to be a primary facilitator in addition to Pete. The final area of judgment related to the design of *learning activities* for the retreat, which were highly interactive in contrast to the didactic methods used in previous retreats.

Location

The primary interest of improving organizational communication was furthered with the selection of the location for the retreat. In Pete and Joan's January 17 planning document, which they used that day in their meeting with the president, the issue was stated as, "Do we plan an overnight retreat out of town, or do we try to meet locally and have half a day plus a day on site?" As they went into the meeting, Pete and Joan felt it should be out of town, although the downside was cost and "taking that many key roles out of the company at the same time," Joan said. To improve communication and build teamwork, Pete and Joan felt strongly that the participants needed to be removed from their work setting, where the problems existed. This was especially important because they envisioned the retreat as an environment in which the participants could temporarily have more equal roles. The location was such an important issue that they broached it with Jones as early as the January 2 meeting, during which they asked, "Should we look at an overnight retreat, or should we do something in town?" As Joan recalled, Jones said that "overnight would be great." So when they formally brought up the options of in town or out of town during the January 17 meeting, they were not surprised that Jones said "out of town" with no discussion. The president had been involved in the negotiations about all important issues for the retreat, and the location was no exception.

Schedule

The actual days on which the retreat would be held were not central
to the primary interest of improving communication. The major
question here, as stated in Pete and Joan's January 17 planning
document, was, "Do we schedule the retreat for a Thursday after-
noon/Friday or for a Friday afternoon/Saturday morning?" Neither
planner believed that the actual days would make a major difference
in furthering the primary interest; Joan personally preferred Thursday and Friday because she wanted to be home with her family on
the weekend, whereas Pete preferred Friday and Saturday "because
it won't be as difficult to staff the management of the company."
Because this judgment did not involve negotiating about the primary interest, Pete engaged in planning practices that furthered his
interest in strengthening the human resource function. Specifically,
he met with three of the other vice presidents to find out what they
thought; the finance vice president recommended Friday and Saturday because the participants "won't miss as much work time, and
it will be easier operationally." Two other vice presidents recommended Thursday and Friday because "we work hard enough, people want to take their Saturdays." Consulting the other vice
presidents helped give them a stake in the retreat and more exposure
to Pete's ideas about management education. Pete was able to present the vice presidents' two viewpoints to the president at the January 17 meeting. According to Joan, Jones "just said Thursday/
Friday. I mean he didn't bat an eye, he just said it."

It was not until after the January 17 meeting that Pete and
Joan "started playing with the schedule and started talking about
time frames and agendas and what would work." By this time, they
had decided on the major areas of content in consultation with
Jones; now the two of them alone negotiated about the overall
schedule. The major question was the relationship of the executive
adventure to the remainder of the program. As Pete explained, "If
we do executive adventure, would we do that in the afternoon before
and then come back the next day and try to reinforce it with small
group interaction? Or should we do executive adventure second?"
By the time of the March 6 meeting with George, they were able to
say that executive adventure was going to be held on Thursday

afternoon and that he was not responsible for it. They asked him to help them come up with other exercises to make Friday morning more interactive than lecture. By circumscribing the areas of the program in which George was allowed to negotiate, Pete was able to maintain control over the primary goals.

Instructors

In order to further his interest in strengthening his function within the company, Pete decided to be a facilitator during the retreat. However, he knew that because of his ongoing relationships with members of the audience, he would need to hire facilitators from outside the company in order to further the primary interest of improving organizational communication. He did this by selecting the consultants from Executive Adventure for the Thursday afternoon session and George as the facilitator for the Friday morning part of the program. Pete and Joan turned to the consultants because they needed people from outside the company to help "break down the barriers and relax the group so that the group would really give honest feedback," said Joan. As Joan and Pete explained, many department directors and supervisors work together every day but "they don't really know each other." Pete also needed an outsider for the Friday sessions to bring some credibility to the process. Another reason that Pete selected an outsider for the Friday sessions was that "I've got some critics, and that's one reason I thought to have a neutral person who has a good reputation."

Although Pete's decision to use an outside facilitator was a result of negotiating about the primary interest, his selection of George from the three people interviewed was a result of negotiating about the other two interests. Joan and Pete interviewed George before the February 13 meeting with the president, partly to ensure that George was available and willing to work on the retreat. As part of their desire to reorient management education, they needed to make sure that George understood their values and objectives in regard to the interactive nature of the retreat and that he would be comfortable with them. In the interview, Pete and Joan said that they were "not looking for the expert, we were looking for the facilitator to help the group learn themselves." By selecting someone who shared these values, they tried to ensure that the negotiation about the structure of Friday morning activities would proceed without conflict. Pete's selection of George also was important in furthering his third interest, of building support for his function in the company. Pete said of the interview, "One green light I felt was that he had just met with the president and executive vice president about something different. And it had been a fairly positive experience with them." Thus, George would add some credibility to the retreat, and therefore Pete's role in planning it, "because he has some recognition in the community so that the president and vice president would buy into the selection of George," Pete said. All this made for smooth negotiating at the February 13 meeting when Pete recommended and the president approved hiring George.

Learning Activities

Pete and Joan strongly believed in the importance of using interactive learning methods at the retreat, in contrast to the highly didactic approach used in previous retreats. Interactive methods would improve organizational communication and further Pete's interest in reorienting management education. Still, this presented Pete with one of the most difficult areas of negotiation. At the February 13 meeting, Pete and Joan negotiated with Jones about using the executive adventure segment, which they were concerned he might not agree to because of his previous resistance. The president agreed to it, Pete explained, because "I think he knows what we can do, and part of his going along with us is he can tell we feel strongly about what we want to accomplish." Likewise, at the same meeting, Pete and Joan explained to Jones more about the interactive nature of the Friday morning sessions, of using a group process to try to promote the skills of a manager's communication. Again, Jones agreed, which was important so they could work with George to plan the specific activities for Friday morning.

Interests and the Evaluation of the Retreat

Although Pete and Joan were critical of certain aspects of the retreat as it unfolded, such as the last part of the Executive Adventure, they believed it was successful. As Joan exclaimed, "I think we accomplished what we set out to do, and I think people had a good time, and I think they left feeling good about it and they want more. I mean, what else is there?" Her positive assessment, that the primary interest of improving organizational communication ("we accomplished what we set out to do") and the interest in reorienting management education ("people had a good time") was based on reactions from participants as well as key members of the top management team. Participants gave generally high ratings to both the executive adventure exercises and the Friday morning program. Pete and Joan saw further evidence of the impact of the program in the number of requests for follow-up programs. On the evaluation form, for example, thirty-two people asked for help in conducting team-building exercises with their staffs and thirty-six asked for more workshops on "positive communication and follow-through with staff." Joan noted, "We're not where we need to be, [but] we have laid a foundation to build upon."

The reaction from top management was equally positive and demonstrated that the same two interests were furthered. For example, Brad, the executive vice president, called Pete on the Monday after the retreat "to say how well it went and how he enjoyed it and how he had been around the company today and people came up to him and started a conversation who he had never said anything but hello to before the retreat," Pete reported. Pete and Joan were particularly pleased with the president's response, which was that they did an excellent job. Even more important was that Jones participated fully in the retreat activities and spoke passionately in closing the retreat about the importance of "communication and how employees want to be communicated to." Pete believed that the success of the retreat solidified his power among the top management team. For example, Pete was particularly gratified by Brad's reaction to the retreat, given the battles they had had about the 1990 retreat. Pete's perception was that his domain had gained power, that it now had "more support to do what we want to do," a critically important outcome of the retreat.

FOUR

Updating Practitioners
in University
Continuing Education

The College of Pharmacy at State University has offered an annual seminar for practicing pharmacists for several decades. The express purpose of the annual seminar has been to provide practicing pharmacists with an educational opportunity to keep abreast of developments in the profession. With the advent of relicensing legislation in recent years, this event has gained the added significance of helping practitioners meet their mandatory relicensing requirements. Three primary planners worked on this market-contingent continuing education program. Carl is the coordinator of continuing education in the College of Pharmacy and was responsible for managing the development and production of the annual seminar. Bob, Carl's supervisor and director of continuing education for the College of Pharmacy, was involved in many of the planning meetings. Richard, a faculty member at the college, served as program director because his area of expertise, cardiovascular disease, was that year's seminar topic. As Exhibit 4.1 shows, program planning for the next seminar began immediately after the previous year's seminar with the selection of the topic and with Richard's agreement to serve as the program director. Most of the planning, however, was concentrated in the six months prior to the April 1992 annual seminar. This included two meetings with selected practitioners for topic suggestions, as well as planning meetings in which Carl and Richard developed the content sessions and chose speakers for the seminar.

Exhibit 4.1. Program Planning Calendar.

April 21, 1991	1991 annual seminar: "Update on Diagnostic Products and Procedures."
April 30, 1991	Select 1992 seminar topic: cardiovascular disease; Richard agrees to serve as program director for 1992 seminar.
November 1, 1991	First planning meeting in which Carl, Bob, and Richard meet with practicing pharmacists.
January 17, 1992	Second planning meeting in which Carl, Bob, and Richard meet with practicing pharmacists.
January 24, 1992	First draft of seminar topics and tentative selection of topic speakers.
January 27, 1992	Third planning meeting in which Carl and Richard review first draft of seminar topics and selected speakers.
February 4, 1992	Final schedule of seminar topics and speakers chosen.
February 11, 1992	Carl arranges for the production of seminar publicity and program registration materials.
February 25, 1992	Publicity and registration materials mailed for annual seminar.
April 19, 1992	Annual seminar: "You and Your Patient's Heart: Update on Cardiovascular Disease and Therapy."

As the calendar in Exhibit 4.1 indicates, final programming decisions about content and presenters were made in early February so that publicity could be prepared and mailed approximately two months before the April 1992 annual seminar.

History and Institutional Setting

State University's College of Pharmacy is located on two separate campuses. Some of the college's faculty conducts research and teaches courses at the medical school campus in a nearby city. Most of the pharmacy school, however, is located on the main campus of State University where it serves the major undergraduate and graduate student populations. Although continuing education programs are presented at the medical school campus, the Department of Continuing Education is located on the main campus. Much of the continuing education programming is located there as well.

Bob and Carl work on the main campus, and each has had

a long tenure at State University. Bob, who is not a pharmacist, has had a long career in the planning and administration of university-level continuing education. He has been the director of continuing education for the College of Pharmacy for six years. Before that, he had worked in other continuing education capacities at the university for fifteen years and at other universities for about ten years. Carl is a third-generation pharmacist who grew up in a family-owned community pharmacy practice. He was a practitioner for fourteen years before taking his current position as coordinator of continuing education at the college fifteen years ago. Although he occasionally does relief work in a local pharmacy, he said he feels "relegated to life in the ivory tower." Bob and Carl respect each other's abilities and work closely in planning the college's continuing education programs. Bob says that although "I am called the director and he is called the coordinator, we work very closely together. There are certain programs that I take responsibility for, and there are other programs that he takes responsibility for. We keep each other apprised of what we're doing." Carl is responsible for the college's large conferences and thus was the primary planner for the annual seminar. Bob attended some planning meetings in order to stay informed but was not involved in the day-to-day planning for the seminar. As is typical of all their program-planning efforts, Bob sought a faculty member from the college whose expertise was related to the seminar's topic to serve as program director. Richard had been a practicing pharmacist for sixteen years before earning his doctoral degree in pharmacy (Pharm.D.). While this program was being planned, he was in his fifth year as an assistant professor at the college and was preparing to apply for promotion and tenure. Although he said he had "always enjoyed giving in-service presentations before I went back to school," he had never served as program director for any of the college's continuing education programs.

The annual seminars have always had an important place in the continuing education efforts of the College of Pharmacy. As Carl said, "The College of Pharmacy has been an active proponent, supporter, promoter, offerer of continuing professional education, I would say, almost from its inception." From a programming standpoint, Carl said, the annual seminars are organized to provide pharmaceutical knowledge that the practitioner "doesn't already possess so that he can chew on it, so that he can take it and put it back into his practice setting." Richard added that the purpose of this year's annual seminar was to keep practitioners "fresh and up-to-date with new information." But this program was important for other reasons, as the planners were well aware. Asked why this program was offered, Carl neatly summarized the unbroken link between past and present planning efforts for this annual seminar: "Tradition! Tradition!" For several decades, the annual seminar had always taken place in April during the university's alumni weekend. As Bob said, "It's carrying on something that began years ago. This weekend draws alumni back. It's a big deal. We want to have something where people say, 'I came to alumni weekend, and it was really top-notch.'" Carl saw the alumni weekend and the annual seminar as having a symbiotic relationship because the program "is in a sense to showcase the college."

In addition to presenting new pharmaceutical knowledge to practitioners, showcasing the college has included an opportunity for college faculty and practitioners to talk. Bob observed that he had "never seen a faculty like this. They do it because they're committed to public service and continuing education." This also meant, according to Bob, that the exposure of the faculty to the practitioners enabled faculty to bring something back to their classroom experience with undergraduates. Richard concurred. Involvement in the program was important to him because it helped him "get exposure to people I would not otherwise have interaction with" and because "we value our service role to the profession and to the public pretty highly." This interest in continuing education also helped the faculty represent the college as a leader, as Richard described it. Being a leader, Richard said, meant that this program helped "people around the state perceive that we are pretty close [to the] cutting edge of knowledge."

The planners knew that the alumni weekend would draw pharmacists from many specialties. Consequently, they wanted to select a seminar topic that would appeal to the varied group. The importance of the proper topic was painfully demonstrated to Bob and Carl when the previous seminar drew only 43 participants, in contrast to a typical attendance of 100 to 125. Carl attributed this drop-off in attendance to having "tried something new," an update on diagnostic products and procedures. According to Carl, they found out that "diagnostics are not something that grabs the practitioners' interest because they don't diagnose." Having learned that lesson, Carl said they selected cardiovascular disease because "any practitioner would need the information that will be provided in the cardiovascular seminar. It's germane to any practitioner's practice." They based their decision on a statewide survey of practitioners' interests in pharmacy topics and program evaluations from other continuing education programs. According to Carl, no one else was involved in making that decision because "that's one of those unilateral decisions. I think it's called the 'privilege of the position.'" It was at this point that the department appointed Richard as program director because of his expertise. On April 30, 1991, a week after that year's seminar, Bob sent a memo to Richard: "This will confirm our conversation of April 27 regarding next year's annual pharmacy seminar. We would like to have you direct the planning and development of this program. We would like to focus the seminar on cardiovascular disease. You can develop the program as you see fit. You will be compensated for your planning, and if you have a role in the program you will be paid for that as well."

In the fall of 1991, Carl said, "You don't have a program until you have a folder. And I haven't started one yet." In November, he started a folder for the annual seminar to be held the following April because he knew it was "time to start working in earnest. We work on a six to nine month lead time." With the seminar topic and program director settled, Carl appointed a three-person program planning committee of local pharmacists "to tell me what they need in program content," he said. He secured their participation by telephone, following up with a letter giving the formal charge to the committee members: "The focus chosen for this seminar will be cardiovascular disease. Summaries from past seminar evaluations and a statewide survey of pharmacists' perceived needs indicated that this topic is the number one area of interest for practitioners. It will be our responsibility to identify the most beneficial component subjects for inclusion on the program within the time constraints allowed." According to the planning calendar, the program planning committee first met on November 1, 1991. Only two of the three practitioners invited were able to meet with Carl, Bob, and Richard. From this meeting, the first tentative topics and speakers for the cardiovascular program emerged. Because the full range of practice settings were not represented by the pharmacists in this first meeting, Carl decided to have a second meeting in January 1992. At this second meeting with practitioners, the program topics and speakers developed in the first meeting were corroborated and expanded. Carl's folder began to fill with planning documents.

The Program: "You and Your Patient's Heart: Update on Cardiovascular Disease and Therapy"

The promotional and registration materials were mailed on February 25, 1992, for the seminar to be conducted on Sunday, April 19, 1992. The goal of the program was stated on the publicity brochure: "Cardiovascular disease is the number one cause of morbidity and mortality. It is essential that pharmacists possess the most current information on this disease state. This seminar is intended to update and expand pharmacists' knowledge base on this group of diseases." Exhibit 4.2 lists the objectives of this program and the schedule of topics. Because the College of Pharmacy is a provider of continuing education credit approved by the American Council on Pharmaceutical Education (ACPE), this program was given an ACPE Universal Program Number to be used for relicensing procedures. As the schedule indicates, the program was seven-and-one-half hours long, which meant an allocation of 0.75 hours of continuing education units. The registration fee was $75 per participant. A planning budget was prepared based on a projected attendance of 75 people. Actual attendance was 101. Although Carl and Bob had been active in planning this seminar and attended the entire day's activities, they had no official roles as instructors. Their primary tasks were to oversee the logistics and to handle any unexpected events. The program director, Richard, was the moderator and presided over the delivery of the program, introducing each topic and instructor, keeping the program on schedule, and facilitating the question-and-answer periods. In addition, Carl and Bob had given Richard a list of items to orient the participants to the self-assessment inventories, question cards, attendance documentation

Exhibit 4.2. Annual Seminar Schedule.

Seminar Objectives

The participating pharmacist should be able to
1. Describe normal regulatory mechanisms of cardiac output, vascular tone, and heart rate.
2. Describe abnormal events leading to, and symptoms or complications caused by, congestive heart failure, myocardial ischemia, infarction, and diabetic hypertension.
3. List risk factors contributing to congestive heart failure, myocardial ischemia, infarction, and diabetic hypertension.
4. Describe routine treatment for congestive heart failure, myocardial ischemia, prevention of reinfarction, and diabetic hypertension.
5. Discuss modifications of treatment for gender, age, race, and socioeconomic considerations.

7:45–8:15 A.M.	Registration in pharmacy lobby
8:15–8:30	Preseminar self-assessment
8:30–9:15	Normal Physiology
9:15–10:00	Pathophysiology and the Disease State
10:00–10:15	Refreshment break
10:15–11:15	Diagnostic Procedures
11:15–11:45	Question-and-answer session
11:45–12:30	Luncheon in the banquet area
12:30–1:30	Ischemic Disease
1:30–2:30	Congestive Heart Failure
2:30–2:45	Refreshment break
2:45–3:30	Prevention of Reinfarction
3:30–4:15	The Diabetic Hypertensive
4:15–4:45	Question-and-answer session
4:45–5:00	Postseminar self-assessment

---

forms, program evaluation forms, and other important documents and scheduling items that participants would need to have during the program. Richard also served as an instructor for one topic, congestive heart failure.

After registration in the College of Pharmacy lobby, participants entered the main lecture hall, an auditorium with a capacity of approximately three hundred people. The first fifteen minutes of the program were allocated to a "preseminar self-assessment," in which the participants completed a fifteen-item inventory of multiple-choice questions that specifically addressed the scheduled topics. Because the theme and goal of the program were to "update and expand pharmacists' knowledge" about cardiovascular diseases, the self-assessment inventory helped participants gauge their current knowledge of seminar topics. Such inventories are also typically required for ACPE program certification.

In order to update pharmacists on cardiovascular diseases, the program was to provide them with "the most current information of this disease state." The content objectives stipulated that the update include a review of normal cardiovascular physiology, which was used to introduce the main topics of the program: abnormal events leading to heart failure, risk factors associated with heart failure, routine treatments for heart failure, and treatment modifications based on specific patient considerations. With one exception, all content was presented by assistant or associate professors with doctoral degrees in pharmacy who taught and conducted research in the College of Pharmacy, either at the main campus or at the medical school campus. The one exception was a medical doctor from the state medical school who presented on diagnostic procedures. Instructors addressed the participants from a podium on the stage. As the schedule indicates, each person had forty-five minutes to one hour to cover the assigned topic. Typically, they lectured for the assigned period, often using overheads, slides, and motion pictures to supplement and illustrate their talks. All instructors but one distributed handouts of their lecture materials or overheads. In the one case in which handout material was not available, Carl and Bob obtained the materials and forwarded copies to the participants in the week after the seminar. The final fifteen minutes of the seminar were devoted to a "postseminar self-assessment" in which participants responded to exactly the same inventory of questions they had been given in the preseminar self-assessment. Participants then tabulated the raw difference between the two scores and anonymously submitted the gain-and-loss scores to Carl at the end of the program. The seminar convened on time, followed the projected schedule, and concluded at 5 P.M. with the completion of the program evaluations.

Interests and the Annual Seminar

This section returns to November 1991 and explains the three interests that Carl, Richard, and Bob were negotiating as they planned the annual seminar. The primary interest was to maintain and enhance the college's position as a leader in the pharmacy profession. This interest was shared by all the planners and, to a large extent, by the practicing pharmacists. Also, the economic interests of a market-contingent education program had to be negotiated. Both Bob and Carl continually represented this in the planning process. Finally, there were the regulatory interests of the pharmacy profession, as represented both in the accreditation of continuing education providers and the licensing requirements of the state. Bob and Carl were the primary representatives of this interest as well.

Maintaining and Enhancing the Leadership of the College

The program planners maintained and enhanced the leadership of the college by presenting the college as the provider of the most current information, by cultivating alumni interest in the college, and by using continuing education programs to showcase the college and its faculty to both alumni and nonalumni pharmacists in its service area.

The first element in this interest is represented in the planners' adoption of the update model of continuing professional education (Nowlen, 1988). The update model is defined by Nowlen (p. 24) as "heavily didactic short courses [that] pursue the central aim of keeping professionals up to date" in terms of the newest research findings in a field. Nowlen contrasts this with other models for continuing education that focus on affecting professionals' competence or performance on the job. There is little concern about the application of the knowledge in the update model, with the greatest emphasis being simply on the transfer of knowledge from the teacher to the participant.

By offering programs designed to present the most current pharmaceutical knowledge, the college sought to maintain its position as a leading provider of continuing education in the state. The planners saw the college as explicitly producing and delivering the knowledge that pharmacists needed to conduct their practice. The planners were quite explicit about this. The title of the program—"You and Your Patient's Heart: An Update on Cardiovascular Disease"—directly identified the seminar as a vehicle by which practitioners could obtain the latest information about cardiovascular disease. Each planner was explicitly aware of this interest. For example, Carl said that "any practitioner would need the information that will be provided," and he wanted this program to expand the "normal knowledge base" of practicing pharmacists. As Carl asked, "Is there new material presented for which there is very little in the literature?" Richard had the same approach: "In recent years, there's been some better understanding of some of the diseases and also some novel drugs. There was new information that might be surprising, areas where I thought there might be these findings that hadn't gotten out to the grassroots level." The information the practitioners need is produced at the university. Richard described the main campus College of Pharmacy as being close to the cutting edge of knowledge. As Richard said, "We're here to give them [the program participants] a product, and the more product you give them, the better it is." As Carl exclaimed, "Let's give the practitioner something that he doesn't already possess so that he can chew on it, so that he can take it and put it back into his practice setting. I want to expand his knowledge base." Clearly, this interest was shared by practicing pharmacists. One practitioner on the advisory committee said that "because the seminar is here at the school, I expect it to be the most up-to-date information. I expect a better, jam-packed program."

This approach to updating is intricately connected to maintaining the leadership of the college in a second way, by enhancing alumni relations. Asked how the college benefited from the program, Richard said, "Our alumni are proud that we are very active in keeping everybody fresh and up to date with new information. I think it helps alumni relationships by coming back here. It identifies your college as a leader." Bob added that the commitment of the college to public service is important in maintaining alumni connections. He said the current dean is "committed to public service at the university, and we have been able to show him some benefits from our interaction in the continuing education/public service arena. People coming and joining the President's Club, giving some contributions to the dean's account, things like that. So there is a relationship and you can say it came from CE" (continuing education).

In order to attract and bolster alumni activity as well as to continue the leadership role of the college, the program also was designed to showcase the college's faculty (the third element of the primary interest). Carl said the program was "PR for the school. It's another way of tooting the horn of the college by bringing instructing faculty who are expert." Thus, Carl, who represented the college's interests in this respect, wanted the program to demonstrate that "the dean employs competent people." Bob described the connections demonstrating the leadership, professional competence, and alumni relations of the college: "This particular program is carrying on something that began many, many years ago, and it is something that brings our alumni back to the campus. Now with mandatory continuing education, we want to put on a real high-quality program that will be a showpiece for the college" on alumni weekend.

Furthering the Economic Interests of the College

The planners, specifically Carl and Bob, also had to be concerned with certain economic factors that influence the planning of any market-contingent continuing education. Financially, the program had to generate enough income to recover its production costs. Carl explained that his department "is a zero-base budgeted operation. The university does not give this department any money," which meant that this program had to "at least approach a break-even point" financially. In fact, though, the college financially supported the institutional structure of the continuing education department in terms of financing its staffing (with the exception of Carl's position, which is shared with the continuing education center of the university). Carl's remarks referred to the financial necessity for the program "to make budget," which meant that this program had to generate enough income to recover the direct costs necessary to produce it. As Carl described it, "How much does it cost in dollars and cents to get speaker A, speaker B, C, D, E, and F in here? What will be covered, what are your absolute sunk costs, what are your variable costs? How few people can we have and still go?

What is the optimal number to break even?" Thus, attendance expectations and conference fees were a crucial concern. Both Carl and
Bob were acutely aware of how accurate their projections had to be
in order to break even. In this respect, they were dealing with an
explicit ceiling on their registration fees. Bob described it as a "kind
of a rule of thumb and agreed-upon thing among providers of continuing education regionally, if not nationally, that we will offer
CE for ten dollars or less per contact hour. And so, if you're paying
faculty to lecture in CE programs and you have all your promotional expenses and all the on-site expenses, there's not a lot of
money left over." This economic interest in cost recovery was
heightened by the institutional arrangement for Carl's position. As
Bob described it, "Because of Carl's joint staffing arrangement with
the continuing education center, they collect the money. And so we
don't participate in the sharing of the money to any great extent."
This was important because, as Bob said, "We hope that we break
even. If we don't, then we underwrite the shortfall." Because of that
arrangement, the continuing education department had to absorb
losses but could not expect to share any profits.

Meeting the Regulatory Requirements of the Profession

The planners had two sets of regulatory interests to negotiate in
planning the annual seminar. First, they had to design a program
that would meet the requirements of the ACPE, which is the accrediting body in the field. They also had to produce a program in which
participants could accrue as many continuing education hours as
possible to be used toward relicensing by the state. The ACPE had
explicit requirements for accrediting pharmacy continuing education programs. One stipulation required that educational programs
have objectives. "It's part of the criteria for ACPE," said Carl, "that
any advertisement, promotion, brochure-type material contain as
much information as you can get into the targeted audience's hands
by giving them terminal objectives." A second requirement was the
preseminar and postseminar self-assessment inventories. Again, Carl
said, "It's one of those things that accreditation bodies like so that
they have a way of quantifying what you're doing." Planning for
these stipulations was important because the ACPE "does have a

review mechanism, and they will randomly audit one program per year." Meeting the ACPE requirements meant that the annual seminar would be accredited and could pass a random audit. Consequently, participants could use their approved attendance hours to meet the state's mandatory continuing education requirements.

In this state, practicing pharmacists are required to submit thirty hours of attendance at ACPE-approved programs (four seminars) every two years to maintain their licenses. Carl was acutely aware of the effect participant interest could have on the program. The previous year's seminar was six hours long, which, as Carl said, was "very nice for participants." But there was a problem that both the participants and Carl knew had to be fixed. Carl explained it this way: "They show up for a six-hour program, which means if they come back in the fall for the postgraduate seminar, which is another six hours, then you have the two together and they come up three hours short. How are they going to get their three hours?" Carl said that opportunities for gaining the extra hours are numerous, "but if they're going to give up an entire day, they like to get the maximum amount of time in. And I can't blame them." This is precisely what the participant evaluations from the 1991 annual seminar had indicated. Part of Carl's programming strategy was predicated on maximizing the available continuing education hours: "You come spring and fall, and you set your calendar, every six months I'm going to the College of Pharmacy, and I can pick up seven-and-one-half hours." By attending four programs over two years, pharmacists can accrue the necessary relicensing hours. As Carl noted, the seminar is "easier to market" when the participants' interests are accommodated.

Negotiating About Purposes

The purpose of the program was to deliver the latest available knowledge to pharmacists in order to enhance their ability to practice. The negotiations from which the purpose was constructed were largely tacit because there was widespread consensus among all the planners as well as the program planning committee members. Everyone wanted what Bob called a "quality continuing education experience." As one program planning committee member remarked, "Everybody's done a cardiovascular program, but they really haven't been comprehensive." Carl responded, "That's what we want to do." Thus, to meet the interest of maintaining the leadership of the college in the profession, all the planners adopted the update model of continuing education, achieved by presenting to the participants the latest pharmaceutical knowledge available.

The stated purpose of the program, as listed on the promotional material, was to update pharmacy practitioners on cardiovascular disease and therapy: "It is essential that pharmacists possess the most current information on this disease state. This seminar is intended to update and expand pharmacists' knowledge base on this group of diseases." This update was defined by Richard as "new information," particularly information "that might be surprising in the use of the drug for something other than what it was intended for originally." As Richard went on to explain, pharmacists "need to know about all the uses of the drugs that they are dealing with, and they need to know particularly when a person's medical situation might cause a doctor to use some odd combination of drug that seems wrong but really isn't." In this sense, the more knowledge pharmacists had about the latest combinations of drug therapies, the better they would be able to understand the significance of prescriptions for particular patients. Bob concurred; the knowledge presented in the seminar would help practitioners counsel patients because they would know more about why certain combinations of drugs were being prescribed. Carl explained the purpose of the program in this fashion: "They [pharmacists] are supposed to know something. And they are supposed to have a base of knowledge when they open up the pharmacy in the morning. And they are supposed to be ready to use that knowledge. If we enhance his knowledge base, that's our desire." By presenting the program as an update of knowledge, the program met the interest of the college in maintaining its leadership as the major source of new information necessary to professional pharmacy practice.

Negotiating About Audience

For a continuing education program with the goal of updating pharmacists, the audience would necessarily be those practitioners who had access to the College of Pharmacy and needed to meet their regulatory requirements. As Carl said, from the very beginning, the program was designed for practitioners in the state. Indeed, the audience was known before the topic was chosen, for the program had been dedicated to the same audience for decades. Consequently, the planners' negotiation in regard to the identity of the audience was largely tacit. There was no conflict. Although a participant in the program could have been any practicing pharmacist, Bob and Carl's economic interest meant they needed to target an audience such that the likelihood of recovering their production costs would increase. This was accomplished in three ways: by presenting a topic that would be of interest to the greatest number of practitioners possible, by directly connecting the program to alumni activities, and by providing the greatest number of continuing education hours possible so that participants could gain maximum per-seminar credit for their attendance.

Carl had said from the beginning that he wanted a program topic "germane to any practitioner's practice." In selecting members of his program advisory committee, he had picked representatives from several pharmacist groups: mass-merchandizing discount pharmacies, community-based pharmacies, hospital pharmacies, and nursing home pharmacies. By consulting with representatives of these various groups, Carl checked his and Bob's perception that cardiovascular disease was of sufficient general concern to attract a large number of pharmacists. Carl maintained throughout his planning activities that selecting the right topic was crucial to having participants attend. "You have to hit the interest," he said, "you have to have something that will bring the people in." This also addressed the need to draw a sufficient number of participants to recover their costs.

The second component of targeting the audience for the program was connecting it to the alumni weekend activities. As we have already reported, the pharmacy program had traditionally been a significant element in the alumni weekend activities. As Carl explained, the annual seminar was designed for "the practitioner who is bringing his family back for alumni weekend. While he's here, take advantage of a postgraduate continuing professional education program." The program brochure made explicit the connection between the two events; it advertised the program and the alumni weekend activities. The brochure was a crucial component of the promotional campaign, for Carl used the college mailing list of approximately six thousand area pharmacists, thirty-five hundred to four thousand of whom he estimated were alumni. As Carl said, connecting the seminar to the alumni weekend was a marketing ploy to increase program attendance, which in turn increased the likelihood of recovering production costs. In addition, mailing the brochure to such a wide audience met the planners' interest of maintaining the leadership profile of the college. Although less than 2 percent of the target audience was expected to actually attend the program, the brochure kept the efforts of the college visible to the other 98 percent of practicing pharmacists.

The third component in attracting a sufficient audience had to do with producing a program that maximized a participant's accrual of mandatory continuing education hours. Carl knew from the start that this program had to be seven-and-a-half hours long. One reason for the smaller attendance at the 1991 annual seminar, in addition to its specialized topic, was its short hours. Fewer hours of credit would have reduced the potential audience for the 1992 program and thus reduced the likelihood of its producing enough income to recover its production costs.

Negotiating About Content

In planning the content for this program, two major judgments were made. The first had to do with the overall topic of the seminar and the second with the specific topics instructors would be invited to address. In both situations, the primary interest of maintaining the educational leadership of the college, particularly in reference to adopting the update model of continuing professional education, meant that the content of the program was chosen to allow the college to demonstrate its pharmaceutical expertise. Essentially, the list of topics and potential instructors, not written objectives, represented the content for the annual seminar. The objectives for the program were not written until they were needed for the brochure, which occurred at the beginning of February. The written objectives were necessary to meet ACPE guidelines and thus were constructed by the planners to meet the regulatory interests.

Part of the function of the program planning committee, which Carl convened in November and January, was to verify that cardiovascular disease was a valid topic in terms of having broad appeal. One of the first questions that Carl asked the planning committee at the November 1 and January 17 meetings was, "Do you think a program on cardiovascular disease states will be overdone?" One response was, "It sounds good." Another committee member indicated that while other opportunities for learning about this topic had been available, she expected the cardiovascular program at the college to be more comprehensive because the others had been "too short to really cover the subject well." Thus, the content of the program was chosen before the program planning committee was convened, and part of the purpose of its meetings was to verify that Bob and Carl had a topic that would enhance the leadership of the college and attract a large audience. The planning committee's main function was to suggest specific subjects to be presented at the annual seminar. The interest of maintaining the leadership of the college can be seen most clearly in the selection of program topics from these suggestions. The topic discussions from each meeting and the final agenda for the seminar show how content choices were predicated on providing fresh information to practitioners.

At the end of the November 1 planning meeting, Carl summarized the committee's suggestions for program topics:

> Ok, we start off. Normal cardiovascular function, the anatomy and physiology for approximately one hour. Diagnostic procedures, surgical procedures for one hour. Risk factors, modifiable. Smoking, cholesterol, the controversy there, bringing in your diet, your age factors, the drug therapy, even talking about drug screening for cholesterol. Hyperlipidemia, hypercholesterol, go to lunch. That's a full morning. After lunch, we're coming back in with risk factors continued and picking up on essential hypertension. New therapies, new thoughts. New approaches to step care,

which is now *bubble care.* You're discussing ACE in-
hibitors, calcium channel blockers. Then you take a
break, then back in for the prevention of myocardial
infarction, prevention of reinfarction, and then some
discussion of some of your drug therapies.

Carl finished his summary with a question that captured the
essential interests: "How much of that would be review for you all,
and how much would be new questions answered?" Leadership
would be maintained if the college provided information that practitioners did not have. One member responded, "The only thing
that would be truly review would be the basic anatomy and essential
hypertension." Thus, the program, as it began to emerge from the
November 1 meeting, was being defined by how new to practitioners would be the topics to be presented.

During the second planning committee meeting on January
17, Richard at one point gave this summary of the suggestions:
"Start with anatomy and physiology, then disease states and patho-
physiology, then diagnostic procedures, then risk factors, choles-
terol-lowering agents and methods, nondrug and drug methods,
treatment in special groups, treatment of special groups." As program director, Richard acknowledged his key interest with his
follow-up comment on the list of topics: "I think what I would do
is not even talk about traditional therapy, [but] talk about the newer
therapies in congestive heart failure." When one committee member
suggested that congestive heart failure is in "almost every third
magazine you pick up," Richard responded, "Well, I try to focus on
[the newer uses], that's where the real exciting news is." Again, the
interest in updating practitioners and thus enhancing the leadership of the college was crucial in determining which topics were
chosen.

The final program as constructed (see Exhibit 4.2) directly
represented most of these topics, as summarized by Carl and
Richard. To understand the significance of these choices, though,
it is necessary to look at what was suggested but not included. For
example, in both planning meetings, the topic of monitoring and
measuring blood pressure was suggested by committee members,
either with respect to being able to actually measure blood pressure

(in a workshop format) or being able to interpret unusual readings (through a case study format). While the planners gave serious consideration to these suggestions for some time, blood-pressure monitoring ultimately was not included because, as Carl said, "This is more of a didactic program. This is more of a learning than a manipulative or hands-on or development-type of program." Another suggestion that arose from the planning meetings but eventually was discarded was a presentation about "modifiable risk factors" with respect to smoking and cholesterol. Carl succinctly described why this topic was dropped: "We were also discussing risk factors that were modifiable. There is enough information, both in the professional press and in the lay press, so that anyone who reads anything knows that you are a fool for smoking [and] you should change your dietary habits." In other words, this is not new information. Furthermore, with respect to cholesterol issues, there was still too much debate—that is, not enough certainty—as to the proper course to follow to minimize congestive failure. In fact, although general risk factors such as smoking and cholesterol disappeared, the idea of special factors affecting heart health remained in an innovative manner. As Richard described it, "You could broaden it to special populations. Special considerations in special patient groups such as age, race, and other things that modify physiology." And that was how the topic presentations actually were structured, with drug therapies connected to disease states and each speaker addressing "age, race, sex, socioeconomic lifestyles within their therapeutic specialty" and how they "would modify standard treatment for these different" groups of patients, according to Richard. Thus, by using an innovative arrangement to present a generic topic germane to all practitioners, the planners sought to enhance the leadership of the college in continuing education as well as assure an audience large enough to recover their production costs.

Negotiating About Format

The planners made judgments about four aspects of the seminar format. All three interests affected the planners' judgments. With respect to the negotiation about *learning activities*, the issue hinged on didactic versus interactional methods. The selection of *instruc-*

tors depended on choosing faculty members who would represent expertise in the specific topics. The essential issue negotiated in regard to the *schedule* of the program depended entirely on the interest in meeting relicensing requirements. The *location* of the program, about which there was never any open discussion, was a function of the planners' interest in showcasing the pharmacy college on alumni weekend.

Learning Activities

We have tried to show how the dominant interest of maintaining leadership was best exemplified in the planners' use of the update model. In terms of learning activities, this interest was central in settling on the two instructional methods that were used: didactic presentations by experts and question-and-answer sessions. The two methods, however, were selected from negotiations on the part of the planners because members of the planning committee, and even the planners themselves, often suggested and discussed interactive and alternative learning activities. Workshops and other interactive activities were early and consistent points of discussion throughout the planning of the annual seminar, yet they never appeared in the final program.

In the November 1 meeting, when the planners were first soliciting for discrete topics for the cardiovascular program, Richard asked whether the practitioners had numerous customers "coming into the store to check their blood pressure." After receiving an affirmative answer, Richard asked whether "we could spend some time teaching people how to detect blood pressure." One committee member responded, "Yes, very definitely!" and another responded, "What if we have short workshops?" It immediately became apparent, however, that some participants would already know how to read blood pressure and would therefore require an alternative activity. Carl and Richard were willing to retain workshops as an option, but "it would be at the tail end of the day," not a central feature of the program. Carl and Richard felt such an activity would "suffer" because "there's not going to be any participation." At this point, the practitioners were beginning to agree; one commented, "I wouldn't say forty people" would participate.

Carl concluded the discussion by saying, "I think that could be a topic we could easily let go." But the possibility of using a workshop format did not go away. The interactive interests of the practitioners surfaced again during the second planning meeting on January 17. In that meeting, workshops on blood-pressure monitoring and cholesterol screening were again considered. One practitioner suggested workshops on operating blood-pressure-monitoring devices and interpreting the results: "It's just that some people have never done it, and I just thought that it might be something interesting for them to learn if they got out there in the field and wanted to think about doing something like that." It was also in this context that a committee member suggested using case studies as a learning activity: "That might be interesting since we're out in the field, if you've got some case studies and you run into contact with some of these things, then you have a better idea of what you look for in the future." But, as before and for the same reasons, the workshops and other interactive learning activities were tabled.

The planners continued to negotiate about the issue of didactic versus interactive learning activities. When Carl and Richard met on January 27 to review the topics and select speakers, they were in virtually total agreement about the topics and their arrangement on the schedule. But there was a problem. With the final array of topics before them, Carl realized that they did not yet have a program that was seven and one-half hours long. They were still ninety minutes short, so Carl once again brought up the idea of using blood-pressure workshops to fill the time. Richard responded with a key statement of interest: "I don't think it's worth a workshop" because blood pressure had become a secondary topic under diagnostics and "might be a little awkward" without the necessary preparation. The solution was to add another didactic presentation in order to have enough instructional time in the program. A panel question-and-answer session, in which participants could ask for clarification of lecture material presented during the program, would complete the day. So, in terms of learning activities, the program began as essentially a didactic presentation and ultimately was presented in that form to the participants.

Why did this program not contain any interactive learning

activities when the planning committee members and the planners at times seriously considered their use? Devoting a large segment of the program to procedural issues rather than new drug therapy would have detracted from the essential purpose of the program, which was to update practitioners' pharmaceutical knowledge. Carl was quite clear about this when he and Richard were discussing eliminating the workshops: "I agree. I think we have, one, not enough time, and two, I think we have too much material to cover." Getting as much new information as possible into the program was the stronger curriculum interest at this point. The program had to be didactic because the primary goal was to maintain the leadership profile of the college by giving practitioners new information.

Instructors

Selection of presenters for the annual seminar, particularly with respect to using the update model and showcasing the college and its faculty, also demonstrates the primary interest in maintaining the leadership role of the college. It explains why the instructors had to be college faculty. Using outside instructors would not have demonstrated leadership or showcased the college. To maintain the leadership of the college, the planners sought to provide the most current pharmaceutical information. In order to update practitioners, the planners had to turn to the faculty of the college because they were the ones most likely to have the information and the ability to dispense it. We have already seen how this interest led to the didactic instructional format. In Carl's planning practice, once topics were defined, he typically began the search for instructors: "Who can best address the topic that we want addressed?" In this case, however, it was clear that the college faculty would best represent that expertise and maintain the leadership of the college as an educational provider. But Carl added another key statement of interest when he remarked that because "this is the annual seminar, I do like to highlight or spotlight the on-campus faculty, the faculty within the college." Why was this important? Carl again expressed some key goals for the program: "It's PR for the school. It's another way of tooting the horn of the college by bringing instructing faculty who are expert." The college maintains its leadership by using its faculty to present new information to practitioners. Thus, Carl and Richard selected presenters who could address the specific topics they had outlined in discussions with the planning committee. The interest in cost recovery also helped produce the final slate of presenters. To recover their costs, Bob and Carl could afford only so many instructors. By using college faculty, the planners were able to project exactly what those instructors would cost because they were governed by university salary regulations.

Schedule

The leadership and regulatory interests were central to constructing the schedule for the annual seminar. The number of program hours can only be understood in light of the interest in relicensure. Scheduling the program for alumni weekend was part of the leadership interest of showcasing the college and its faculty.

Carl often described his planning practice as a balancing act, which meant he frequently had to negotiate different interests. With respect to the number of program hours, the regulatory interest that made a seven-and-one-half-hour program necessary was more important than the feasibility of planning content: "It's much easier to schedule a six-hour program than a seven-and-a-half-hour program." In a planning process generally characterized by considerable consensus, the number of hours became quite a serious issue at times. From the very beginning, Carl had to continually keep the relicensure requirements at the fore in the planning process. According to Carl, Richard's concerns "lie primarily in structuring a strong program from the standpoint of information." Carl, on the other hand, had several interests to represent. The primary one here was having a program long enough (defined in this context as seven-and-one-half hours) to help participants meet relicensing requirements. This negotiation became crucial during the January 27 planning meeting in which Carl and Richard were structuring the final program so that publicity and registration materials could be produced and disseminated. During this planning meeting, Richard and Carl agreed almost totally on the program from 8 A.M. to 3:30 P.M., at which point they ran out of content. Richard could have concluded the program at that point, but Carl knew he had to have another hour and a half. That was when Carl again suggested blood pressure monitoring workshops, and Richard responded, "I don't think it's worth a workshop." He meant that new information was more important for this program than teaching procedures, although he added, "We can put it in if you feel strongly that we need it." But it was not the topic Carl was concerned about; it was the length of the program because, as he said, "We have this period at the end of the day." Richard and Carl negotiated a solution to this dilemma by adding another didactic presentation, concluding the lectures with a question-and-answer period and ending the program with the postseminar assessment. By adding another didactic lecture to update practitioners, the planners deftly accommodated the leadership interests represented in the update model. In adding pre- and postprogram assessments (and counting these activities as part of the seminar schedule), Carl accommodated the interest in complying with ACPE accreditation requirements and arrived at a seven-and-one-half-hour program. As Carl said, the tests gave him "thirty more minutes, legitimately."

The second important element of the schedule was to hold the seminar during the college's alumni weekend; a main feature of the weekend was an open house for the College of Pharmacy. As Bob explained it, "Well, this particular program is carrying on something that began decades ago, and it is something that brings our alumni back to the campus. Now, with mandatory continuing education, we want to put on a real high-quality program so that it will be a showpiece for the college for this particular weekend." So, while the actual program schedule was decided primarily on the basis of the regulatory requirements, the planners set the seminar for alumni weekend because of their interest in showcasing the college, its faculty, and its leadership.

Location

During all the planning meetings to which we had access, there was never any discussion of where the program would be held. From the very beginning, it was assumed by all planners, as well as the planning committee, that the program would be conducted in the lecture auditorium of the college, despite the availability of a modern continuing education center five minutes from the college on foot. Indeed, the seminar used the dining facilities at the continuing education center. But the negotiation about the location was consensual for several reasons. First, having the program located physically at the college and in conjunction with the alumni weekend open house directly met the primary interest in maintaining leadership by showcasing the college. The program really could not have been held anywhere else and still have met these goals. Furthermore, although Carl's salary was also paid by the continuing education center, it was in the financial interest of the college for cost recovery not to use the continuing education center any more than necessary because of the added expense. Thus, by locating the program on the actual premises of the college, the planners enhanced the image of the school, maintained and encouraged alumni relations, and maximized their chances for recovering production costs.

Interests and the Evaluation of the Annual Seminar

Carl and Bob believed the program was a success. Program costs were budgeted for a break-even attendance of 75. With 101 participants, the program's income met all direct costs for speakers, travel, promotion, supplies, food services, and ACPE fees. The number of participants was also significant because, as Bob said, pharmacists "are only four months into the [two-year] relicensure period," which meant the planners' choice of topic had been an important element in attracting participants. Another measure of the importance of the topic was Carl and Bob's impression that they probably "did not lose 15 people all afternoon." In fact, most participants were still in the lecture hall after the program officially ended. Bob and Carl felt that the topic was timely. Bob thought, "We really hit the mark on this one." Carl concurred: "It was subject matter, it was presenters, it was something very relevant to a practice environment." As Carl concluded, "When you have participants still with you after you have officially adjourned, it tells me one thing: the subject matter and the presenters are hitting a target that is near and dear to the conferees' heart. We had that room full at five o'clock." In addition, on the day after the seminar, Carl reviewed the participants' program evaluations. "I did not see a single no to the question, 'Were your personal objectives met by this seminar?' Traditionally, we hit in the mid-nineties, but on this one we did not have a single no." Carl also reported that all the raw scores on the pre- and postseminar self-assessments were gains, which indicated that participants' knowledge of cardiovascular disease and treatment had increased. As Carl said, practitioners "are supposed to have a knowledge base [and] be ready to use that knowledge. If we enhance his knowledge base, that's our desire." So, from economic, attendance, knowledge, and participant-evaluation perspectives, Carl and Bob felt the program had met the goal of providing practitioners with current information about an important topic. There were indications that the program met certain institutional interests of the College of Pharmacy. The dean had come to registration and had welcomed the participants. Bob noted that the dean was "pleased with the attendance," and Carl reported that the dean had said it was "a dynamite program." In addition, Bob reported that "one emeritus faculty member, who is also in charge of fundraising told me that he had two contacts for the President's Club . . . [that] resulted from just casual conversation at a coffee break." Thus, the annual seminar not only helped maintain the visibility of the continuing education efforts of the college, it also met the goal of maintaining alumni connections with the university.

FIVE

Promoting Social Change in Community-Based Education

The Organization for Persons with Disabilities (OPD) is a federally funded organization, the mission of which is to reduce the incidence of developmental disabilities and to improve the quality of life of people with developmental disabilities and of their families. For Ann, the OPD director, community-based educational programs were an important means of accomplishing this mission. Thus, she readily accepted a proposal from one of the organization's professional staff members, Marti, in the summer of 1991 to develop a program to help employers meet the requirements of the Americans with Disabilities Act (ADA), which was to take effect in 1992. Marti was the primary planner for a one-day program titled "Meeting the Challenges of the ADA." The program, which was scheduled for November 1991, was canceled because of insufficient enrollment. As Exhibit 5.1 shows, the program planning took approximately four months, lasting from the middle of June, when Marti first began discussing the idea, until October 10, when the program brochure was mailed. As the primary planner, Marti held two meetings with Ann to obtain approval for developing the program and to review its major elements. Because this was one of the first programs she had planned for OPD, Marti had one meeting with the technical assistance coordinator to learn the logistics at OPD for planning a community program. Her final public meeting was with the

Exhibit 5.1. Program Planning Calendar.

July 26, 1990	U.S. Congress enacts the Americans with Disabilities Act of 1990.
January 2, 1991	Marti hired as program coordinator at OPD.
June 6, 1991	Marti discusses with other OPD staff idea for a program about ADA for employers.
June 27, 1991	Marti receives approval from Ann to plan the program.
July 16, 1991	Marti meets with Connie (technical assistance coordinator) to discuss the process OPD uses for planning community programs.
July 26, 1991	Rules and regulations for the ADA published in the *Federal Register.*
August 28, 1991	Marti meets with Ann to review tentative program schedule and budget.
September 12, 1991	Marti meets with all instructors.
October 10, 1991	Program brochure mailed to target audience.
November 6, 1991	Marti and Ann decide to cancel the program.
November 14, 1991	Scheduled date for "Meeting the Challenges of the ADA."

instructors to orient them to their task. The program was to be held at a local hotel in the same city as OPD.

History and Institutional Setting

The federal government funds in every state an OPD to enhance the quality of life for citizens with developmental disabilities and for their families. According to the Developmental Disabilities Act of 1987, under which OPDs around the country are funded, people are referred to as having a *developmental disability* if they have a mental or physical impairment that is manifested before age twenty-two and will continue indefinitely. Further, these impairments must result in substantial functional limitations in three or more of the following activities: learning, mobility, self-care, language, economic self-sufficiency, self-direction, and capacity for independent living. Although OPDs must be administered by a teaching hospital or a university, they can be located anywhere within a state. The OPD in this case, which had been in existence for twenty-five years, is located on a university campus.

The system of OPDs around the country was created to take a particular human rights stand with respect to people with disabilities; this OPD is no exception. The organization is an advocate for people with disabilities and provides them with training that promotes independence, productivity, and integration into the community. The OPD is involved in four types of activities in carrying out its mission: education and training, direct services to people with developmental disabilities and to their families, consultation to other service providers locally and nationally, and dissemination of information and research to increase public awareness. Although university courses provide some education, community-based outreach programs produce 75 percent of the OPD's participants annually (more than 4,500 people in the past year). Most participants attend programs cosponsored by the OPD and community-based service agencies, government agencies, or consumer advocacy groups. Particularly relevant to this case study is that the OPD had never sought to provide programs to the business community. Ann and Marti used the opportunity presented by the ADA to work as advocates for people with disabilities in a new market, the workplace.

The OPD received from its funding agency a core annual budget of $600,000 for its current three-year funding cycle; it used the money to "leverage" (attract) other resources to support its basic mission. Its seven full-time and five part-time professional staff members were supported by the basic grant, as well as by additional grants and revenues. Ann had been the director for two years and was beginning to prepare the proposal to the federal government for the next three-year cycle, which would begin in October 1992. Ann had hired Marti at the beginning of the year as a program coordinator. Although she had been at the OPD for only six months, Marti had a rich background in the disability field as a rehabilitation counselor. A lively and energetic individual, she was also uniquely positioned to be aware of the issues the program is designed to address. Not only had Marti "had lots of work in personnel and salary administration and managed one hundred employees but I am also sitting in a wheelchair with a closed head injury I've recovered from, visual limitations, and a learning disability as a result of a closed head injury," she said. During the first six months of her employment, Marti had been heavily involved in writing grants and providing technical assistance to service agencies. With the upcoming implementation of the ADA, she had proposed to Ann ideas for two community programs for which she would take primary planning responsibility. The first was a statewide program to explain the implications of the ADA to pharmacists, and the second was the program reported in this chapter. Although Marti had planned programs before, these were the first she had planned for the OPD.

On July 26, 1990, the United States Congress created Public Law 101-336, the Americans with Disabilities Act of 1990. Modeled after the Civil Rights Act of 1964, this law establishes "a clear and comprehensive prohibition of discrimination on the basis of disability." Lawmakers expected the act to bring massive changes to society because their findings state that forty-three million Americans have a mental or physical disability that is covered by the act. The scope of disabilities covered is comprehensive and includes orthopedic, visual, speech, and hearing impairments, infection with human immunodeficiency virus (HIV), cancer, heart disease, mental retardation, emotional illness, specific learning disabilities, drug addiction, and alcoholism (Bulbin, 1991). Congress found the law necessary because many people with disabilities have been discriminated against in employment, housing, public accommodations, and education. Title I of the act, which deals with employment issues, applied to all employers with twenty-five or more employees as of July 26, 1992. It specifically prohibits these employers from discriminating against a "qualified individual with a disability" in all phases of the employment process, including job application procedures, hiring, promotion, compensation, and training. Employees meet the definition of "qualified individual" as long as they can perform the "essential functions" of the job, even if they cannot perform some of its less important functions. Further, employers can be required to reconfigure the job or make modifications to existing physical structures to accommodate a person with a disability.

Marti saw the need for this program with great emotion and clarity. Having been active in the disability community for many years, she knew that the ADA would have a profound effect on her professional and personal life. National mandates like this come along only once in a generation, and she was eager to aid in its implementation. Although most provisions of the law would not take effect for one year, she had been besieged by employers asking for help in dealing with it. In her view, the situation was "kind of like right after a tornado, a lot of people need roofers." She believed that many employers "are afraid that this is going to put them out of business. They think that everything they do will be very expensive. That any accessibility modification is going to be thousands of dollars. That they are going to have to hire people who cannot do the job." In response to this situation, a number of other national programs about the law had already been held, costing anywhere from $500 to $2,000. However, her sense was that "a lot of employers cannot afford to send their personnel director to D.C., they can't justify it." She felt, then, that a program offered by OPD could "diffuse a lot of fear attached to this legislation [and] get the information to them at a cost they can afford."

The time period from Marti's first thought of holding the program until she received Ann's approval for OPD sponsorship was three weeks. The idea occurred to her in a discussion with Michael King, an OPD staff member who would ultimately be an instructor for the program. Marti and Michael served on the Mayor's Committee on Disability Issues and were talking about "what we could do other than just have the annual employer/employee of the year award luncheon. We felt that not only could we educate human resource professionals about the legal requirements of ADA but also advocate for a fuller inclusion of persons with disabilities throughout their organizations with such a program," said Marti. However, they both felt that getting such a program approved by the local government would be difficult and time consuming and that they could move faster through the OPD. Nothing much happened until June 26 when Marti ran into a human resource director from a local industry who told her, "We have so many questions about the ADA. We don't know where to turn to get information." This was the final push for Marti to seek OPD sponsorship for the program. She went to work the next day and "hung around until five, and I waited for Ann to come downstairs," at which time she explained her idea for the program. Ann "asked me a couple of questions about where it would fit in, agreed that

it could fit, and told me that my next step would be to arrange it
as a cost-recovery program," Marti recalled.

As the program planning progressed, the ADA was making
its way into the national media. The regulations on how the act
would be implemented one year later were published by the federal
government on Friday, July 26, 1991. During the next weekend, a
series of television reports covered the near panic among employers
in reaction to the guidelines. Ann noted the historic nature of this
law: "The ADA is bringing with it tremendous societal changes.
And I don't think very many people understand yet how large a
societal change comes with this piece of legislation. I think that as
people begin to understand, their first reaction is fear. It's fear for
companies that they are going to go bankrupt because they can't
possibly do this." Because of the importance of the new law to the
disability field, Ann believed that the OPD had to do something in
response. The organization did so by offering a program about the
law for directors of personnel and human resources in public and
private workplaces.

The Program: "Meeting the Challenges of ADA"

The program was scheduled to last all day Thursday during the
second week of November and was expected to attract fifty to
seventy-five people. It was to be held at a local hotel within two
miles of the OPD office. Marti expected that most participants lived
within a two-hour drive of the site and would not require sleeping
accommodations. Because participants would arrive at the site in
the morning and leave immediately after the program, she would
start late enough (9 A.M.) and end early enough (4:15 P.M.) not to
make the day too long for them. The cost of the program was $75
for those who preregistered and $85 for those who registered on the
day of the program. The fees would cover program attendance,
lunch, and two fifteen-minute beverage and snack breaks. Exhibit
5.2 shows the program schedule, much as it appeared on the brochure mailed to the target audience. Although there were no written
objectives for the program, its content was described in the brochure. All participants would be together for all sessions. Except for
the luncheon speaker and the closing panel, all instructors would

Exhibit 5.2. Description and Schedule for the ADA Program.

Program Description

This ADA-response program is designed to enhance human resource managers' skills in developing a positive agenda for both their employers and persons with developmental disabilities. Participants will review the substance of the regulations and its definitions, acquaint themselves with defenses against alleged discrimination, and explore the differences and similarities in ADA and existing legal provisions such as the Civil Rights Act and Sections 503 and 504 of the Rehabilitation Act of 1973.

Seminar Agenda

9:00–10:30	Nuts and Bolts: What the ADA Is and Is Not *Margaret Greeno*, attorney
10:30–10:45	Break (coffee, juice, pastry, and muffins)
10:45–11:30	Breaking Through the Glass Ceiling: Planning Career Paths for Employees with Disabilities *Jane Lowe*, OPD
11:30–12:30	Not for Wheelchairs Only: Planning for Physical Accessibility in the Workplace *Marti*, OPD
12:30–1:30	Buffet lunch *Sharon Stevens*, executive director, Governor's Council on Developmental Disabilities
1:30–2:15	Smoothing the Way: Working with Existing Employees to Promote Positive Interactions with Employees with Disabilities *Michael King*, OPD
2:15–3:00	Beyond 9 to 5: Social and Recreational Programming That Includes Employees with Disabilities *Beverly Jones*, OPD
3:00–3:15	Break (lemonade, sodas, fresh fruit)
3:15–4:15	Panel question-and-answer-session • Where to look for qualified employees • How to analyze a position • Job restructuring and the ADA • Sources of technical assistance

give a formal presentation for most of their allotted time, leaving some time at the end of their sessions for questions from the audience. The luncheon speaker, a politically important person in the state in the area of developmental disabilities, had been asked to speak for fifteen to thirty minutes about the government's perspective on implementation of the ADA. The final panel would be composed of all the day's presenters, who would respond to questions from the audience. The brochure indicated that in addition to the formal sessions, all the instructors would be available throughout the day to answer questions that participants might have. Marti knew all the instructors personally and recruited them for the program; Ann recruited the luncheon speaker. Of these five primary instructors, three were people with disabilities (Margaret, Marti, and Michael) and two were African-American (Jane and Michael). In addition to being the primary planner, Marti was one of the instructors. Except for the lawyer who led off the program, all presenters were staff members at OPD.

Interests and the ADA Program

Marti negotiated about three major interests in planning the program about employing people with disabilities. These interests were shared by all primary actors in this relatively small organization. The primary interest was to seek social change in the way people with disabilities are treated. Although the program focused on employers, the interest encompassed advocating social change on a variety of fronts. Another major interest was the mandate from the funding agency for ODP to use allocations to leverage more funds to carry out the institutional mission of OPD. The third interest was to enhance the image of the OPD in its larger institutional context and in the community.

Advocating Social Change

Marti and Ann clearly saw the work of the OPD as connected to a larger social movement that works to produce social change for people with disabilities. They repeatedly stressed this; as Marti said, "It's really important not to segment the work of the disabled advocate community." This interest had two important features: a focus on advocacy as opposed to only providing information and an emphasis on systemic change as opposed to only educating individuals. When Ann took over as director in 1990, the basic philosophy of OPD was moving toward a stronger emphasis on advocacy and away from only providing information. As she says, "Information is less important than attitude and general comfort level. It's irrelevant if you know how to meet the needs of someone in a wheelchair if you do everything in your power to keep them out of your place of business." The importance of and need for advocacy is one of the "real challenges of the disability field; we tend to be more sophisticated with our information than with how we go about and really make some pretty substantial societal changes," Ann said. Marti shared these views of the organizational mission—to work as advocates "*with* persons with disabilities," Marti said. "And we think the *with* is important so that we are not just representing them because we know what's best, but we are working with them to facilitate their representation."

The focus on creating systemic change flowed directly from Ann and Marti's view that "people with disabilities are our core constituency. Anything we can do to make systemic change, the better. The bottom line of whether we are effective is the impact it has on those clients," said Ann. She pointed out that this view was not simply a function of the personal beliefs of the people who were employed by OPD. She explained that whenever OPD considered an educational program, it had to clearly have a "multilayered effect, that is not just 'this will help John Jones do a better job,' even though we would like to help John out. The feds are very clear about this. They don't want us focusing on John; they want us focusing on changing systems." The mission of advocacy affected all activities of OPD. Ann strongly believed that everything done in OPD, "whether it's in-service training or technical assistance or creating a videotape, carry with it a statement of values of this program." The organization was unambiguous on this point. It was not in the business of just helping people know how to best serve people with disabilities. It also wanted to change people's attitudes because it is "more important to want to have those individuals as employees in their businesses and their school classrooms" than to simply provide techniques for helping people with disabilities, Ann said. Marti echoed this sentiment by saying, "We do have a specific social action viewpoint to express about inclusion. We are upfront about where we stand, and we feel that we cannot fulfill our mission as an OPD in a value-neutral environment."

Perhaps the most telling expression of this approach was in OPD's actual management practices. Ann explained that this interest carried over into her own organization because she had tried "very hard to put our money where our mouth is, related to issues of disability and minority and cultural groups." OPD had struggled in trying to provide a model of how an organization can deal with these issues, because it was a part of a larger organization that was "not very sensitive to these issues," Ann said. Ann recalled a particular incident to illustrate this point. For a significant period of time, OPD had a staff member who could not use the bathrooms in the office because they were not accessible and so had to use the bathroom in the building across the street. When Ann reported this situation to the people in the larger organization and asked them to make the bathroom accessible, their responses ranged from "Couldn't you find other office space for this individual?" to "How long is this individual going to be working there?" This had been a tremendous learning experience for OPD: if the organization was not grappling with issues of discrimination against people with disabilities, "we would fail to appreciate what other agencies are going through as they do this," Ann said.

Leveraging Resources

A fundamental interest that pervaded all OPD activities was the need to generate sufficient financial support to carry out its work. Ann succinctly summarized this interest in describing their funding: "We, in essence, receive money from the federal government that is to be used as administrative support to leverage other dollars." All staff members understood this need; as Marti explained, "Our job is to leverage money, which is about the same thing as capitalism. We're supposed to take a little and make a lot." Leveraging resources was necessary for the very survival of OPD. As Ann said, "The federal government provides us with eight or nine *Federal Register* pages of things that we absolutely have to do. And then they give us the money to do about a quarter page worth. In essence, the message to us is 'Go, ye, and leverage.' And we are judged on all of the pages, even though they are very upfront that they don't give us money to do that. We are to be out working with the state to build resources to make these things happen." Because the core dollars were not to be used for adult education activities, the agency had to leverage other resources to carry out these programs. According to Ann, "Our mandate from the feds is that one of the areas [in which] we are to develop programs is adult education. But we are not to do that as such with federal money. We are to do that through leveraging any other resources we can." An example of this was the work of OPD related to the ADA, which did not even appear in the list of activities mandated for the agency because the ADA became law after the current funding cycle began. Yet Ann believed something had to be done because the funding agency "would think it somewhat curious that one of their programs ignored a big change in the status of people with disabilities in the country." As with many other activities, OPD had to use existing resources to leverage other ways to support its ADA-related educational programs.

The funding problem was manifested in Ann and Marti's first concern—not to lose money on any program—and, second, to generate a surplus that could be used to support other OPD activities. Ann was clear about this: "One of the first considerations in any activity we take on is, How is it going to be paid for? . . . In essence, there is no money to lose." This was well understood by Marti, who knew that "not losing money is what is driving this program." In this context, leveraging resources meant having a staff member use her time, paid for by core dollars, to develop a program. Direct expenses had to be recouped from fees generated from program participants. Thus, while Ann expected the programs to break even, she typically counted only "our out-of-pocket costs, not all of the staff time and in-kind" costs, she said. A direct example of leveraging resources for use in other activities was that Marti planned to use the surplus income from the ADA program to support other educational programs. In her first planning meeting with Ann, Marti said that "with any profits, I would still like to do something that is more of our advocacy work, which we can't support by charging fees on something for parents or something for teachers."

Enhancing the Image of OPD

Fundamentally, Ann and Marti viewed their educational programs as part of a long-term strategy to maintain visibility and credibility in the state. Of immediate concern was Marti's interest in enhancing the image of OPD within the employment community, a new audience for the agency. She saw the ADA program as a way to "get ourselves out into the community of employers as someone with a degree of expertise." Marti believed that even those who received the brochure but did not sign up for the program would be inclined to look to OPD for future work. As she said, "One of the fastest ways to buy credibility is to make people pay for a program. So this is a way to get our name out there without beating our own drum." Marti wanted to "get our foot in the door, establish ourselves as regional experts, and then we can continue to spread the gospel about ADA." The interest in enhancing the OPD image also had a potential financial payoff because the program would have been worth doing "even if we just break even, between the added enhancement of our public image plus the possibility of additional consulting in the field," Marti said.

The OPD also had an interest in maintaining its visibility and credibility with its parent organization, state and national funding agencies, and its other clienteles. Ann noted the importance of enhancing the image of OPD within the parent organization: "We still have visibility issues on the university campus. Every time we do something, we try to let the administrative structure know that we are contributing to the public service mission." In addition to Ann's interest in enhancing the image of OPD internally, she argued the necessity of its being "a visible force within the state that aligns itself with certain values." Ann was explicit about how the educational programs of OPD are affected by this visibility: "When we select a mailing list that we use for any given endeavor, in addition to targeting those people we really hope will come, we also have a section of people we target for a different reason. And that is to inform them of what we are doing, to better assist them in understanding who we are." So Ann wanted "state agency people, Disability Council people, consumer and advocacy groups to look at this program and say, 'This is kind of nifty.' And to hold that in mind."

Negotiating About Purposes

The purpose of the program, which was negotiated about primarily by Marti and Ann, was stated in the brochure: "to enhance human resource managers' skills in developing a positive agenda for both their employers and persons with disabilities." The decision was largely consensual because both planners shared the interest of advocating social change and of enhancing the image of OPD. Marti and Ann's negotiation about these two goals in the ongoing work of OPD created the program, which opened new territory for the agency, and gave the program its advocacy orientation. Why and how did OPD decide to sponsor a program on the ADA, which was being done for the first time? On the surface were reasons not to focus the efforts of the agency on a law that would not go into effect for a year. Although Marti indicated that "personnel people would call me up or catch me in a meeting and ask about the ADA issue," no one had collected data systematically that would suggest that employers felt a need to learn about the ADA. In fact, Marti was clear that a discussion with a single human resource manager asking her a "ton of questions about the ADA . . . moved me to take a chance on my program idea." Marti recognized the risk in this decision when she observed on July 8 that the program would respond to "a real unmet need, possibly before those with that need are aware of it yet." Further, Ann clearly stated that responding to the ADA was not in the three-year plan of OPD. Thus, Ann and Marti had no formal organizational mandate to plan a program that would educate employers about the ADA.

Despite the lack of systematic data and a formal organizational mandate, it was clear to both Marti and Ann that OPD should sponsor the program. As Ann explained, what Marti came up with is "very much in line with our overall philosophy and mission. So it was a definite fit." It was a good fit because the planners and the organization shared the interest of promoting social change for people with disabilities. Both Marti and Ann saw the ADA as the most important piece of civil rights legislation ever passed in regard to people with disabilities. So, while the ADA was not in the three-year plan, Ann noted that "we've got to be responsive to the field, which is changing way too fast to not reshape, as you go along, what needs there are in training." Leading by running a program about the ADA would also enhance the image of OPD, particularly in terms of its funding agency. Marti expected that the program "would give us visibility both within our community and with the national OPD organization, our funding parent." Ann was even more explicit: "They would wonder about an agency that allowed a major piece of legislation like this to happen without in any way addressing it or being interested in it."

Marti and Ann's primary interest of advocating social change was reflected in the program in a second way. While the program focused on information about the law, its most important aim was to enable employers to use the law for the betterment of people with disabilities. Clearly, Marti had a "specific action viewpoint to express," as she put it, because she chose not to work through the city government, the leadership of which might "demand more neutrality than we wish to show." Thus, the purpose was not to simply inform human resource managers about the law but to enhance their "skills *in developing a positive agenda*" [emphasis added] for both workplaces and people with disabilities. This statement of purpose was an unambiguous expression of the primary interest; Marti felt "not only could we educate human resources professionals about the legal requirements of the ADA but also advocate for a fuller inclusion of persons with disabilities throughout their organizations." Indeed, she said she wanted to "push, propagandize, that people with disabilities often make better employees." Ann agreed that the purpose of the program was a combination of providing information about the regulations and advocacy for people with disabilities. That their discussions yielded an advocacy approach was not surprising because Ann believed that such an orientation was "very general across all the programs we run." In sum, Marti and Ann engaged in a largely consensual negotiation to offer a program on the ADA that expressed their personal and organizational interest of seeking social change for people with disabilities while enhancing the image of OPD.

Negotiating About Audience

On October 10, the OPD staff mailed brochures to 215 human resource managers who work in companies with more than one hundred employees located within about a sixty-mile radius of the OPD office. This group constituted the target audience, about which the planners made two judgments. The first involved the selection of human resource managers, a new audience for OPD. The second judgment involved the extent to which the audience would be consulted in constructing the program and, by extension, informed about it.

Who Should Attend

Given the interest of OPD in working as an advocate for and with people with disabilities, it was natural that Ann and Marti were able to select the new audience with almost total consensus within the agency. Of course, the imminent implementation of the ADA was central to this decision because, as Marti pointed out, "for the first time there are some real teeth in the law to make a fair effort toward nondiscrimination in their hiring. This will bring a new sphere of influence that the OPD has not been active in up until now." Indeed, passage of the law made it imperative that OPD begin to address the potential employers of people with disabilities if it was going to advocate social change. Marti clearly articulated how the primary interest of OPD was manifested in selecting the audience: "Instead of addressing people through their disability organizations, saying, 'Here are your rights,' we are going to be working directly with people who do the hiring. So they are aware of the rights too. Because some people don't represent their rights very well in every situation." Thus, in the planners' view (in Marti's words) OPD could not continue to only educate professionals "who directly provide services to people with disabilities, like social workers, caregivers, and rehab people." OPD needed to work with employers "to open up the market to let them compete equally without fear on the employers' part."

Marti also explicitly set the program up as a way to leverage resources. With the passage of the ADA, Marti believed the agency was in a position to provide a needed service to an audience that could pay for it; any surplus income would be available for other purposes. In her words, instead of "giving a lot of free advice, we should start making some money on it." In explaining the rationale for this new audience to Connie, technical assistance coordinator of OPD, Marti argued that the program was being "aimed at human resource personnel because they are the ones coming in with the requests. It just seems ridiculous that we do this as a freebie when the budget situation demands that we recover costs for it." Some additional revenue might come not only from the money generated by the program but also from "consulting business for the OPD from some of these same people who ask specific questions," Marti thought. Thus, the selection of this particular audience pushed the agency's agenda of advocating social change and created the possibility of leveraging resources to fulfill the mission in other ways.

Involving and Informing the Audience

Except for a handful of people who had contacted Marti personally about the need for the program, the 215 people in the target audience were not aware of the November 14 program until they received the brochure in mid October. Obviously, then, no members of the audience were involved in negotiating about the purpose, content, or format for the program. It is important to understand why the planners used this approach when an alternative would have been to involve the audience actively in the planning. Marti clearly had the evidence and a suspicion that the audience might not recognize its own need for the program. While she was planning this program, Marti was planning a similar program about the ADA for pharmacists. In her planning meeting with Connie on July 16, she explained that the pharmacists "did not know that their establishments fell under the ADA provisions." She felt the same way about the human resource managers for, on July 8, she indicated that "we seem to have identified a real unmet need, possibly before those with that need [the human resource managers] are aware of it."

The planners negotiated over two interests in constructing this relationship with the audience. Marti was so invested as an advocate for the core constituency of OPD that she believed that the audience would have a similar interest and thus simply had to be informed about the program in a mailing in order to attract registration. Marti negotiated over this interest in a planning meeting with Connie on July 16. Marti asked Connie whether running the program in mid November would be "too short a time line." Connie said, "Yes, I really do." Then Marti argued that because some provisions of the law would go into effect on January 26, 1992, the perceived need for the program would be so great that "to meet the timing of it, we have to accelerate because they need to have this information." Connie acquiesced and essentially sealed the belief that the only relationship needed with the audience was a one-time mailing because of the urgency of the topic. This decision was also supported by the interest in enhancing the image of OPD. Ann and Marti both felt strongly that just announcing the program would yield secondary benefits, namely that, in Ann's words, "the OPD is here as a resource for people who have questions about the ADA." Thus, the very act of informing the audience about the program would enhance the image of OPD as a resource. Any relationship with this new audience was more than the OPD had had in the past and constituted a good beginning for future efforts.

Negotiating About Content

Marti had constructed the content for the program with little assistance from anyone else in the agency. As she said, nobody else "was involved in a decision-making role, although for input I've bounced ideas off some people." Objectives were never written; content was expressed in terms of topics and instructors. By July 29, Marti said that "most of the speakers and topics are figured out." The only content judgments left were "what order it's going to flow in to maximize the learning process. How long the segments are going to be. Who is going to cover what so there is no needless overlap," Marti said. When Marti met with Ann on August 28 to review the content, she outlined the speakers and topics, order of presentation, and time allotted for each instructor. Ann gave her approval for the program, saying, "It looks like it's falling into place." Thus, Marti was ready to hold a meeting with the instructors on September 12, the primary purpose of which was to make sure that "we don't infringe on each other's territory," she said.

Marti negotiated about all three interests in constructing the curriculum. To advance the primary interest, it was important that the content represent an advocacy orientation in regard to people with disabilities. Marti ensured this by selecting instructors she personally knew would take an advocacy approach to the topic, all but one of whom were staff members at OPD. In fact, nearly all content was expressly a reflection of the specialties of OPD staff members. In other words, except for the opening session by the attorney, the content was based on who was available to participate from among the OPD staff.

All three interests converged: by using OPD staff members, who did not need to be paid, Marti could run a low-cost and low-risk program (interest two) and could enhance the image of the agency by showcasing the areas of expertise (interest three). The primary goal of advocating social change was clearly expressed in the content of the program. Although the content could have been a day-long update on the provisions of the ADA, it was not, except for the opening session by attorney Margaret Greeno. Marti said Greeno was to cover "a brief synopsis of what the ADA is, what dates different things go into effect, and what the legal defenses outlined in ADA are." Marti was clear about the interest driving the remainder of the program: "What we hope to get across to people is not just 'here's what the law says' but also how to make the law work. We can do a lot to promote the employability of persons with disabilities and promote not just entry level jobs but really give these people a fair shake at a career ladder." This orientation was evident as each instructor explained his or her focus at the September 12 planning meeting. For example, Beverly Jones, who would speak on social and recreational programming, commented that "changing attitudes also occurs in a recreational setting." The advocacy orientation was central to all the content to be offered in the program.

Advancing the primary interest did not necessarily mean that the content had to be derived almost exclusively from the expertise of the OPD staff. Marti could have developed potential topics first and then chosen instructors from outside the agency who had an advocacy orientation. However, Marti also had to negotiate about the other two interests. In terms of the second interest, using in house instructors who did not have to be paid gave the program a greater likelihood of success because it would need fewer registrations to break even and it could generate more surplus income (an obvious way to leverage resources) for funding future programs. In terms of the third interest, Marti explained, "I want to show people that in the OPD itself we have a broad range of consulting expertise. So that's one consideration." Although Marti obviously could have enhanced the image of OPD simply by putting on the program, using the agency staff as instructors was a much more forceful expression. How Marti selected Jane Lowe, whose topic was planning career paths for employees with disabilities, was an example of how Marti negotiated all three interests to construct the content for the program:

> Some of them [OPD staff] volunteered when they heard me talking about the program. Jane, for instance, has a desk next to mine, and when I was working on an earlier grant for ADA, she asked to sit in. And then we had a couple of more conversations, and I said, "Do you want to do this program? Do you have something that would fit in?" She said, "Yes, I've done four or five ADA lectures around the country, and I have a pretty good idea of what needs to be said." So I said great, here's someone in-house that I can plug in. If not, I might have to go elsewhere for a speaker. I cannot afford to risk on this first program, this whole new venture area.

Thus, in Marti's words, the three interests "all tie together" so that it made sense to construct the content around the expertise of the OPD staff.

Negotiating About Format

As Marti negotiated about the three major interests, she made important judgments about four areas of the program format. The most important judgment in regard to the *schedule* was whether the program would take one or two days. The judgment about the *location* in which the program would be held was related to the cost of using the facility and its accessibility for people with disabilities. The selection of *instructors* was connected to their assocation with OPD and the extent to which they would present a good mix in terms of race, gender, and disability. Finally, there was little discussion about the program's *learning activities,* which were to be primarily didactic.

Schedule

A major feature of any program is its length because it limits what can be accomplished. Marti was well aware of this and early in the planning had considered the benefits of a two-day program. She clearly linked this to advocating social change. On July 8, she explained, "I am probably going to try to do it as a two-day, as an overnight. Just so that I can bring enough people with disabilities in to interact casually with these folks to try to get some of the attitudinal change that I want." She believed that the purpose of the program should not be simply to provide information about the ADA to the audience but also to change attendees' attitudes so that they would want people with disabilities in their organizations. She believed these could be better accomplished in a longer (two-day) than a shorter (one-day) format. Although this was important to Marti, she and Connie decided on a one-day format at their July 16 meeting, which focused on orienting Marti to the logistics of planning a community education program for OPD. A conversation between Marti and Connie shows how the economic interest (the need to leverage resources) strongly affected the final outcome:

Connie: It's a one-day?

Marti: I've got it listed as possibly an overnight. It probably could be cut to a one-day.

Connie: I think it would be better to cut it.

Marti: Do you think it would get better attendance with a one-day?

Connie: Yeah, and there would be less expense.

Marti: And that way I could just cover food at breaks and a luncheon.

Connie: Right, right.

The interest that Marti and Connie were negotiating about is clear. Connie believed that the program would be more successful financially if it were one-day, because the attendance would be greater and there would be less risk of losing money on a canceled program. Of course, greater attendance would generate more surplus income that could be used for other OPD efforts. Although the shorter program was certain to reduce the likelihood of creating attitudinal change, Marti concluded that "keeping the cost down to encourage participation in a one-day program is preferable." Her judgment, then, was to accomplish what she could in a one-day program rather than risk having no program at all.

Location

There was never any question among the planners that the program would be held in the city in which OPD is located. The central judgment Marti had to make was which hotel facility to book. After considering several facilities, she selected a hotel about two miles from OPD. Two important interests converged in terms of the data Marti collected in regard to the hotel choice. She collected information on the cost of various facilities and their accessibility to people with disabilities. Costs included meeting space rental and meals. As Marti explained her preference for a particular hotel to Ann at their August 28 meeting, "We want to use this hotel because they've got the best price. They beat the other hotels by almost 100 percent. They are providing more for less money." The price was important because any savings in this area would become surplus income to be used for future programs. Marti said that with this particular hotel, she also "worked out a deal to allow the program to be canceled at the last minute without penalty and for us to be billed for everything after the fact." This was important because it meant that no money had to be spent before the program was held. Holding the program in an accessible facility was equally important because Marti believed strongly that the program had to exemplify social change (interest one) in deed as well as word. In other words, the program could not be held in a facility that was inaccessible to people with disabilities. Marti underscored the importance of this consideration when she recalled that after delegating the task of finding a hotel to another staff member, she had to "recall all the hotels because [the other staff member] almost booked us into a nonaccessible facility." Thus, Marti selected the hotel not only because of the economic interest but also because "it can handle accessibility requirements better than the other facilities," she said.

Instructors

As discussed earlier, the economic interest was a prime consideration as Marti selected instructors for the program. This was one way to keep the cost low and thus increase the income surplus. Marti explained to Ann in an informal meeting, "The beauty of the program is its ability to test the market waters at minimum cost to the OPD since all but one speaker comes from in-house." Thus, Marti used in-house staff members for several reasons: they had the necessary expertise and an advocacy orientation (interest one); they did not have to be paid, which increased the likelihood that the program would leverage additional resources (interest two); and they would showcase the OPD to a new audience (interest three).

An equally important consideration in selecting the instructors was that they be people with disabilities and be diverse in terms of race and gender. In orienting the program to social change, Marti explicitly assembled a set of instructors such that "there is significant involvement by people with disabilities and people who are minorities so that we don't just have a bunch of white males in suits standing up there and lecturing. . . . Michael is a quadriplegic. Margaret's a juvenile diabetic with a closed head injury. I have a closed head injury and use a wheelchair. And we also managed to bring in a black woman, a black male, a Hispanic woman, and two white females. We try to balance our programs." Marti saw the presenters with disabilities as essential to achieving attitudinal change among audience members: "Studies in changing attitudes toward persons with disabilities always point to two things. One is that you have to interact one on one with the person with the disability. But the second is that you have to see them as equal or superior. And by using people with disabilities as presenters and then the casual interactions over meals, we do think we'll have a greater impact than just sending an able-bodied person up there to speak to them." The selection of the instructors was another example of how Marti negotiated about the social change throughout the program.

Learning Activities

The most notable aspect of the selection of learning activities for the program was the relative silence on this issue throughout the planning. However, the lack of discussion, in combination with the structure of the day's activities, suggest that the learning activities would have been primarily didactic, with the possibility of some time for questions at the end of the presentations. As stated on the brochure, "Presenters will be available to answer questions from participants after the training is completed." This format, the didactic presentation, was a direct expression of the third interest, enhancing the image of OPD. It was important that the program showcase the expertise of the OPD staff, and an obvious way to do this would be to give each staff member a short period in which to tell the audience what he or she knew about the topic. Their talks could generate questions during the breaks and after the session, which Marti planned for. Marti also commented that "in the future this [format] will lead to some other consulting business for the OPD from some of these personnel directors who ask specific questions."

Marti's program-planning practices also influenced the format. The day would begin, as Marti explained to Ann at their August 28 meeting, with "about an hour and a half for the attorney's lecture" about the legal aspects of the ADA. OPD staff members then would have four sessions of forty-five or sixty minutes in which to make their presentations. By giving them a relatively short amount of time, the implicit message to the instructors was to offer didactic presentations. This was also the explicit message that Marti gave to them during the September 12 planning meeting. Almost the entire meeting was taken up with reviewing the main points of their presentations, except for a brief mention of the format for learning activities. Even while appearing to give the instructors permission to use a variety of learning activities, Marti put no structures in place to accomplish this. As she explained to them, "Right now, I've got everything set up in a classroom format. I'm thinking of breaking it out to banquet format, which would let you, if you wanted to do something wild like give them an assignment to work on as groups and report back, fine." In other words, the instructors could stray from the norm ("do something wild") by asking the audience to perform an assignment in small groups.

Interests and the Evaluation of the Program

On October 30, "Ann and I sat down and agreed to make a final decision on the program next Wednesday [November 6]—we need ten registrations or we cancel," Marti explained. Although Marti expected to attract fifty to seventy-five participants, if only ten people attended, "we would have changed the room layout and made it a more informal workshop," she said. Marti and Ann canceled the program during their meeting on November 6. At that time, two people had registered for the program; two more registrations arrived later in the week. Although the deadline for preregistration had been set as November 8, Marti and Ann did not believe that sufficient numbers of additional people would register in the next two days. Marti had always recognized that cancellation was a possibility; she had explained to Ann at their August 28 meeting that OPD was not risking much money: "I think we are going to get more than enough enrollment that we are not going to run into a problem. We won't get into much money from the OPD just in case I miscalled this, and on November fifth we find out we have three enrollees." Although Marti said that "it would have been nice if we had the attendance," neither she nor Ann was discouraged by the cancellation. As Marti reflected on the cancellation, she said, "I think everybody worried more than me about my potential mental health if we didn't get the attendance because I seemed fairly vested in this program. But I am more vested in the secondary benefits that I saw coming out of it than the actual program." Her reasoning about the importance of the secondary benefits was that "because we are in a social change environment, we have all these secondary goals for which the program is just a vehicle. And we managed to get most of those accomplished."

The secondary goals were the three interests about which

Marti negotiated in constructing the program. In terms of the first, both Ann and Marti believed that planning the program created many opportunities for future programs that would carry on the social change agenda of OPD. As Ann said of even this specific program, "The training will eventually be done. The preparation will serve us well in terms of offering this training in the future." In particular, they had evidence within a month of the cancellation that their planning efforts had opened a new market, the employment sector, for their social change agenda. Ann explained, "We have put ourselves in a position to be a provider of technical assistance to individual businesses and organizations. Once the awareness level increases some, we will probably joint-sponsor with some folks who have expressed an interest." Marti was able to provide specific examples of how the publicity for the program opened up the new market: "The Chamber of Commerce has talked to us about doing a program for them, and the local restaurant association is talking with us about doing a program for them." Ann clearly saw that the efforts of OPD in regard to the ADA would be the mechanism by which the agency could push its social change agenda with this new audience. However, "It's a new audience that we still have to learn about," Ann said. "I'm not sure it's an audience that responds to a piece of paper received in the mail from an unknown group. When looking at the people who did respond, they tended to be from businesses that had some awareness of our program, which says to me there probably needs to be more personal groundwork laid." As Ann saw it, informing the new audience about the ADA was a necessary first step in the efforts of OPD to advocate social change. "The pieces of paper that came across the desks of people who did not register still created that first little bit of awareness that we can follow up on," she said. "So I think it was positive just to get some public relations materials out with our agency associated with the notion of assistance for ADA."

Although both planners hoped that their work would leverage resources for other programs in the long term, the program brought in no money for OPD in the short term. As Marti evaluated this aspect of the program, she said, "Any money we made we would have plowed into another program. I do regret not being able to do that other program. I'm going to look for some other money for it." Further, the time that Marti spent on the program was not spent on other work (such as grant writing) that might have leveraged resources. However, neither Marti nor Ann believed that the money spent on direct expenses was significant. "Printing and postage costs totaled less than $50, and Ann considers the payoff on PR [public relations] at least equal to that. So, technically, we didn't lose anything," Marti said.

Both Marti and Ann believed that the image of OPD had definitely been enhanced by all the publicity given to the program, particularly in terms of the full-page articles that appeared in the two local newspapers about Marti and her work regarding the ADA, including the workplace program. Ann's evaluation was that "the publicity that occurred from it for us was a real plus. It was well covered by the newspapers, and I think that we increased the community's awareness about the ADA and what it meant. And I think we also increased awareness that the OPD is here as a resource for people who have questions about the ADA." Marti agreed with this assessment: "We've gotten a fair amount of PR out of this. We have higher visibility. Locally, our name is much more tied with disability issues than it had been." Marti had even more direct evidence than Ann about the effect of the publicity because she was the subject of the articles: "I know a lot of people have read the articles because they caught me and told me." Although the program did not take place, Marti's planning practices produced benefits by increasing the visibility of the agency in the community.

Guidelines for
Responsible Planning

Part Three directly addresses the issue of how to responsibly negotiate interests in organizational relationships of power. Our central
argument is that pragmatic planners must be able to read organizational power relationships in order to anticipate conflict and
provide support in carrying out a vision of planning that is substantively democratic. By substantively democratic, we mean to move
beyond the formal techniques used in democracies (such as voting).
Rather, planners' attention should be focused on practices that allow all people affected by an educational program to have a substantive role in constructing the curriculum.

Planners need to act according to a political analysis of their
organizational context. This is the focus of Chapter Six, in which
we argue that responsible planners have to anticipate how power
relationships can support or constrain their efforts. The chapter
provides an interpretive framework for anticipating power relationships, thereby setting out explicit guides for planners' actions.

In Chapter Seven, we present an ethical standard for planning. The central ethical question in planning is, Whose interests
will the planners represent in constructing an educational program? We draw upon a living American tradition to propose that
planners adopt a substantively democratic process. We elaborate on
this by defining five categories of people whose interests always

matter in planning programs: learners, teachers, planners, institutional leadership, and the affected public.

Chapter Eight addresses the important issue of what planners need to know in order to negotiate among interests responsibly. After an extensive discussion of negotiation as the central activity of planning, we explore the technical, political, and ethical knowledge that planners need.

We conclude the book with a discussion in Chapter Nine about the intellectual roots of our effort to see program-planning practice in adult education and the social sciences as an integration of human action in structurally organized settings. Here, we make our final argument—that planning programs for adults has to be understood as a social practice rather than in terms of an applied science.

SIX

To Plan Responsibly, Be Political

The three cases of curriculum construction in Part Two recall a central truth about planning. It is accomplished in a world of power relationships, some constraining and some enabling, that define the terrain on which planners must act. In order to understand planning practice at all, and most certainly to have any hope of planning responsibly, planners need a working account of how power relationships define planning situations and how they support or threaten a democratic planning process. In this chapter, we reject the dichotomy between rationality and politics often found in the planning literature. In its place, we offer a view of planning practice as a social activity in which the only way to plan responsibly is to act politically. The chapter begins by considering the need for a planning theory that links planning with its social context. The second section reformulates the boundedness of rational planning by offering a framework that ties together power, interests, and action. The final section presents a conceptual scheme for planners to use in interpreting the power relationships and interests in their institutional contexts and the practical implications of this scheme for their work.

Rationality of Planning Practice

Program planners in adult education complain regularly about the irrelevance of theory to their daily practice. Sork and Caffarella

(1989) suggest that they complain either because they take shortcuts in order to get the job done, or because context largely determines how planning is done, or because planning theory is irrelevant to practice. These complaints are made as often about theories in the classical viewpoint (see Brookfield, 1986) as about theories in the critical viewpoint (see Ellsworth, 1989). Planners say, for example, that Knowles's 1980 prescriptions for program planning, which flow from his andragogical assumptions, sound great in theory but do not tell them what to do in the actual situations in which they find themselves. As Forester (1993) points out, this reaction is not so much anti-intellectual as it is a cry from a drowning person thrown a book on water quality instead of a rope. If planners are to be thrown a rope, a theory needs to help them make sense of and act responsibly in the practical organizational realities in which they construct programs. Central to this organizational reality are the historically developing and structurally based relationships of power and associated interests about which planners must negotiate in constructing any educational program. Between the individual actions that program planners undertake and the political and economic structures that provide the backdrop for those actions lie the practical situations in which planners must work.

Clearly, our theory is different from the comprehensive rationality models that dominate the literature, such as that proposed by Knowles (1980). Theories based on comprehensive rationality assume that planners face well-defined problems and have a full array of alternatives, complete information about the context, and unlimited resources to solve these problems. While they offer a potentially appealing direction for planners' actions, these models assume an ideal and neutral stage for planners. The naturalistic models (for example, Brookfield, 1986; Houle, 1972) at least point planners in the right direction by showing that rational action is bounded (or constrained) by context. By simply pointing out the constraints, however, these models still focus on individual action by telling planners to do the best they can given the constraints. While comprehensive rationality models may be irrelevant to helping planners respond to actual situations, the bounded rationality models may actually tie their hands (Forester, 1989). Because these models do not provide a way to distinguish the types and legitimacy of various constraints in actual situations, for example, they constrain planners' responses to whatever works. To plan responsibly, then, adult educators must be able to read a situation so that they can select appropriate strategies for responding.

Power, Interests, and Program Planning

Adult educators always plan programs in contexts defined by a concrete set of power relationships and associated interests. These concepts (power and interests) and their relationship structure planners' action in planning practice. Our central point is this: power is an enduring capacity to act, but it may or may not be exercised on any particular occasion (Isaac, 1987). This distinction, between power and the planner's exercise of it in concrete situations, is crucial because it allows for a distinction between planners' actions and social structure while showing how they are fundamentally connected. It does this by placing educators' actions at the center of power, as the exercise of power; it also places power at the center of educators' action, as the property that makes planning possible (Giddens, 1979; Isaac, 1987). In this chapter, we take up the forms of power relationships amid which planners must act. We argue that planners must distinguish several characteristics of these forms of power in order to plan responsibly. However, although these enduring relationships of power give planners the capacity to act, they still have to exercise that power in a concrete situation. In the language we developed in Chapter Two, negotiation is the exercise of that power, and its success depends, among other things, on the knowledge and skill of the planner. Further, these relationships of power are only *relatively* enduring and they too are subject to negotiation in planning practice. These issues are explored more fully in Chapter Eight.

Power Relationships and Planning

Power is the capacity to act, distributed to individual planners by virtue of the enduring social relationships in which they participate (Apple, 1992; Isaac, 1987). This view recognizes both the ubiquitous nature of power and the social conditions of its existence. First, it is important to understand that power is not a specific kind of relationship, such as that in which one person gets another person to do something he or she would not have done otherwise. Although this is the most common view of power, it is entirely too restrictive because it fails to recognize that all planning practice assumes the capacity to undertake the activity. Rather, power is a capacity to act, a logically necessary feature of all planning practices. To speak of the *power of a planner,* then, is to indicate what planners can do, "where doing is understood as performing a practical activity according to certain understandings and reasons" (Isaac, 1987, p. 76). These understandings, or ends to which action is directed, which we call *interests,* are essential dimensions of power and of action.

The second important feature of a planner's power (or capacity to act) is that it results from certain enduring social relationships. To say this does not deny that individual planners actually possess power or that they exercise it. Rather, it means that a planner's capacity to act is rooted in social conditions (Isaac, 1987). For example, Pete had certain capacities to act because he was a vice president of the Phoenix Company. Certain powers accrued to him *because* of his position, not because of any personal attributes he may have had. For example, he had the power to plan the management education program; while he was able to do certain things because of this power, he was constrained from acting unilaterally because he was in a matrix of power relationships that included the president and other vice presidents. Program planners must recognize that the different kinds of power relationships they encounter call for different responses. (The last part of the chapter presents a conceptual scheme for reading these power relationships.)

Pete's power, which came with his job, was exercised continually while he planned the program. However, the success of his exercise of power was *always contingent* (Isaac, 1987). In other words, Pete had to act within given relationships of power at the company, and whether he would succeed (in the actual negotiation with the president, the other vice presidents, and George) was always conditional (meaning he did not really know how these negotiations would turn out).

Exercising Power in Planning

Exercising power in concrete situations is always a form of negotiation among the people involved (Forester, 1989; Isaac, 1987). It
is not a one-way relationship in which person A gets person B to
do something in some stimulus-response fashion; rather, it involves
some reciprocity among those involved. As Giddens explains,
"However wide the asymmetrical distribution of resources involved,
all power relations manifest autonomy and dependence in both
directions" (1979, p. 149). In this view, power is not something to
be given or taken away because it is always being negotiated. What
bears emphasis here is that stressing that the exercise of power is a
form of negotiation does not mean that conflict is always involved.
Often, if not typically, program planners exercise power in rather
mundane ways. For example, Bob and Carl started out with the
power to select a topic for the annual seminar. Nevertheless, they
had to exercise that power to select a specific topic, cardiovascular
disease, and convince the faculty member (Richard) and the advisory committee that this should be the topic for the 1992 seminar.
The fact that nobody contested the selection shows that the negotiation was highly consensual. But without consent by all parties
involved, plans for this topic could not have proceeded.

To emphasize that the exercise of power should always involve negotiation does not deny that many relationships are forms
of domination in which power is distributed asymmetrically (Giddens, 1979; Isaac, 1987). Planners often find themselves in situations
in which they have power over someone, such as Carl and Richard's
power over the participants in the annual seminar. In contrast, Pete
planned his program in a situation in which the president had
power over him, in the practical sense that all important features
of the program had to be approved by Jones.

Two important points of clarification are needed here. First,
not all relationships of power that planners face are relationships
of domination. In some situations, the capacity to act is distributed
relatively equally to all parties. For example, in negotiating the
curriculum for the ADA program, Marti and her faculty had an
equal say in determining the content that would be taught. An
important implication of this notion is that domination is not a

necessary feature of planning contexts but a subset of all power relationships that a planner might encounter. Nevertheless, most situations are marked by asymmetrical power relationships, and the difficult issue for the planner is to know whether these asymmetries are forms of legitimate power (authority) or illegitimate power (domination).

The second point is that even in asymmetrical power relationships, there is always some form of negotiation in performing the activity at hand. Pete clearly was in a subordinate relationship to the president in planning the management education program. Nevertheless, the structure of president–vice president relationships at the Phoenix Company limited how the president could exercise his power and distributed to Pete real power that allowed for a "variety of modes of leverage, maneuvering, and strategic bargaining" (Isaac, 1987, p. 91) in constructing the program. Although Pete could have tried to use the program to move the company to more participatory forms of management, the evidence is that he decided he could not negotiate this successfully with the president. However, he did use leverage and bargaining, such as when he got approval for his plans from the other vice presidents before going to the president and when he left the executive vice president out of the planning entirely. The important implication here is that power is always reciprocal—the actual construction of the program depended on the negotiation of many key points by those involved. This example acknowledges the existence of preset power relationships, while showing that planners always face the problem of how to achieve their interests by exercising their power. What becomes central to responsible planning, then, are the values and strategies that planners bring to bear in the exercise of their power. These are important because they shape the educational programs and because they play a role in supporting or transforming the power relationships themselves.

Power and Interests in Planning

In Chapter Two we defined *interests* as a complex set of dispositions, goals, values, desires, and expectations that lead people to act in certain ways and to position themselves in a particular manner when confronted with situations in which they must act (Morgan, 1986). In Chapters Three, Four, and Five, we showed the practical connection between the dominant interests of the people involved in program planning and the significant dimensions of the programs they constructed. Here, we elaborate on the concept of interests by showing the benefit of seeing three different types of interests and by articulating the relationship between power and interests in planning practice.

We have made the distinction between relationships of power, which provide planners with the capacity to act, and the exercise of that power in concrete situations. We do not need to know Pete's and Joan's interests, for example, to know that they are vested with certain powers by virtue of their places in the social structure of the company. In other words, they were able to act the way they did because their positions at the Phoenix Company gave them a certain amount of power; the specific interests they held were immaterial to their powers. For example, it may well have been in the learners' best interest for Pete and Joan to decide the content and format of the program. However, Pete's and Joan's relationships of power with the actual learners in the program are not affected one way or another because the planners and learners may have shared similar interests. In sum, there is no necessary connection between the relationships of power faced by a planner and the interests of the actual people involved in the planning process (Isaac, 1987).

However, interests are centrally involved in the exercise of power. All those involved in planning a program exercise their power in accordance with their own concrete interests and thus construct the educational program. For example, Pete and Joan had a fair amount of discretion to construct the management education program because of their power. However, the actual program that resulted from their planning was causally related to the specific interests with which they negotiated in exercising those powers. Of course, to say that the program was causally related to these interests obviously does not mean that the program could not have come out another way because, as we pointed out earlier, the exercise of power is always contingent. It does mean that the construction of the actual program depended on the power of those people whose interests were negotiated, what those interests were, and the outcomes of the actual negotiations that occurred.

Having now argued for the centrality of interests in the exercise of power, we believe it would be fruitful to distinguish among three types of interests that exist in planning practice (Isaac, 1987). *Expressed interests* are the "revealed preferences" (Isaac, 1987, p. 96) that are actually held by particular people in the planning process. (Isaac uses the term *subjective* interests.) An example was Pete's expressed interest in changing management education at the Phoenix Company from an information-oriented, didactic format to a more problem-based, experiential format. Pete's power at the company did not depend on this interest; if he had an expressed interest in using only didactic formats, he would have the same power. However, Pete's expressed interests were crucial in the exercise of his power, the outcome of which was a management education program that was highly participative. Clearly, the program took the form it did, at least in part, because of Pete's expressed interest. Thus, the outcomes of the exercise of power in any planning situation "are determined both by the structural distribution of power *and* the subjective understandings, preferences and 'will' of" the people involved in the process (Isaac, 1987, p. 97).

An *ideal interest* means what is really in the interest or good of a person, whether she or he thinks so or not. (Balbus [1971], Connolly [1972], and Isaac [1987] use the term *objective interest*.) As with expressed interests, ideal interests do not determine relationships of power; they operate within the exercise of power. In contrast to subjective interests, these interests cannot be determined simply by asking people what their preferences are. Rather, they are a function of a person's ethical beliefs about "what forms of social life are just and morally legitimate" (Isaac, 1987, p. 107). Thus, Pete had an ideal interest in educating the leaders of the Phoenix Company to take on more participatory forms of management, even if this did not govern what he did in this particular situation. In fact, when George tried to move the program in this direction, Pete argued that although the company should work toward this goal, it could not be negotiated because of the expressed interests of various people (particularly the president) in this situation. The notion of ideal interests, which are central and explicit in the theories and practices in the critical viewpoint of planning (reviewed in Chapter Two) is a necessary part of any normative theory of planning. We will explore at length in Chapter Seven our proposition that planners have an ideal interest in constructing educational programs by using a substantively democratic planning process. As explained earlier, this interest, while held by some educational planners, does not necessarily derive from an analysis of what planners actually do but from an analysis of what forms of social practice are morally legitimate. Where it is different from other critical theories of program planning is that we argue for the need to connect this ideal interest to an analysis of the power relationships faced by planners in actual settings (Forester, 1989; Isaac, 1987).

Real interests are the norms, values, and purposes implicit in what planners do. In this view, planning practice is a rule-governed activity, and individuals learn the rules and expectations that govern their conduct while engaging in the activity. To be a planner, then, is simply to learn how to perform certain activities and to incorporate this information in working within a particular institutional setting. Thus, real interests can be seen as the "practical norms that govern the exercise of power" (Isaac, 1987, p. 100) in any planning situation. This type of interest is different from ideal interests, which are the purposes to which planners *should* ascribe, because real interests are the norms and purposes that are *actually* exercised in practice (which explains the *real* label). However, using this label does not mean that expressed interests are any less real (Pete's expressed interest did, in fact, influence the form of the program) but rather that certain interests are causal in practice (and can even shape expressed interests), even if the planner does not recognize them.

These three types of interests are illustrated by Pete's planning practices at the Phoenix Company. Pete had an *expressed interest* in reorienting the management education programs to an approach that encouraged learner participation and interaction. Further, he may have had an *ideal interest* in moving the company to more participatory forms of management through the educational programs that he planned. However, he had a *real interest* in strengthening the human resource function at the company, thereby strengthening his power so that he could be more effective at achieving his own interests and thereby improving the company. The satisfaction of his expressed interest had to be tailored to the real interest because he had to be careful not to force a program on the president and vice presidents that was so different that he would jeopardize his standing in the company. Further, because the ideal interest (pushed by George) threatened his ability to strengthen the human resource function, he did not challenge the company's management norms (when he said to George, "We are not ready for this yet").

Finally, Isaac (1987) makes three points of clarification about real interests. First, they are usually implicit, rather than explicitly identified, in actual situations and are generally sustained through habit as opposed to any conscious effort. He quotes Dewey (1927, pp. 159–160) in explaining the importance of habit: "The influence of habit is decisive because all distinctively human action has to be learned, and the very heart, blood, and sinews of learning is creation of habitudes. Habits bind us to orderly and established ways of action because they generate ease, skill, and interest in things to which we have grown used and because they instigate fear to walk in different ways. . . . Habit does not preclude the use of thought, but it determines the channels within which it operates." These real interests, then, are so ingrained in planners' practices that they generally do not consciously recognize them. Second, practicing based on real interests does not necessarily mean that a planner believes that those interests should prevail. Rather, they are the norms that govern practice in a particular institutional setting. Finally, it is important not to assume that any interest is an unchanging characteristic of the person. Rather, like power relationships, interests are always reproduced or transformed in the exercise of power. Thus, interests are constructed, and thus can be reconstructed, in actual planning situations.

Rational Action in Planning: Political
Boundedness of Planning Situations

If planning practice is a social action conducted within varying relationships of power and characterized by the negotiation of interests, what would rational action look like? The answer, in short, is that being rational means anticipating how existing relationships of power are likely to support or constrain a substantively democratic planning process and acting in ways to nurture such a process. In a political world, rationality can only be maintained in practice if program planners carefully assess the institutional contexts in which they work and act according to the structure of the situations that they face (Forester, 1989). Planners do not typically work in situations characterized by symmetrical relationships of power within which all interests are equally important and negotiation proceeds on a consensual basis. Rather, the most common situations are marked by asymmetrical relationships of power that threaten as well as offer opportunities for democratic planning. In response to these common conditions, planners need to understand that responsible planning requires political action. It is simply not possible, or responsible, to act the same in all situations, because what would protect democratic planning in one situation may prevent it in another. This is not a relativistic argument that says that all planning actions are equally valid, nor does it argue that whatever works is necessarily good planning. Rather, it asks planners to assess how a concrete planning situation is socially and politically constructed and how their relationships of power can be exercised to nurture substantively democratic planning.

How to characterize the political boundedness of rational action thus becomes the central problem for any theory of program planning. Planners inherit a matrix of power relationships, and, to be useful, the theory needs to conceptualize the recurring influences planners can expect to encounter. If the bounds that planners face were seen as idiosyncratic to each situation, as most models in the naturalistic viewpoint assume, rational action would be relativistic. Planners would have to make do because they would have no way to anticipate the pressures, threats, and opportunities available to them. However, if it were possible to typify bounds that can be anticipated in any planning situation, doing so would provide planners with a way to act in practical ways that sustain democratic planning. Table 6.1 offers a conceptual scheme that delineates four different ways that relationships of power and associated interests can structure the situations in which program planners must carry

Table 6.1. The Political Boundedness of Nurturing a
Substantively Democratic Planning Process.

Source of the Power Relations

		Socially Ad Hoc	Socially Systematic
Relations Among Legitimate Interests	Consensual	Bounded Rationality 1: Individual Limits *Strategy:* Satisfice	Bounded Rationality 2: Social Differentiation *Strategy:* Network
	Conflictual	Bounded Rationality 3: Pluralist Conflict *Strategy:* Bargain	Bounded Rationality 4: Structural Legitimation *Strategy:* Counteract

Source: Adapted from Forester, 1989, pp. 34, 53.

out their work. Understanding the contingencies of power relationships provides a rationale for the political boundedness of rational action in planning by specifying the situations in which planners must act. The table also suggests corresponding strategic approaches that planners should use to plan responsibly in each type of situation. In other words, the table offers a way to read how the relationships of power and associated interests structure planning situations and offers approaches to guide planners' exercise of their power in these situations.

This view of the boundedness of rational planning depends on a particular political theory, which can be understood when it is compared with other program-planning models. The models in the classical viewpoint see politics as getting in the way of rational planning and offer a systematic set of procedures for overcoming this noise in the planning process. Models in the naturalistic viewpoint assume there will always be bounds on planning, because it always occurs in a context, but see no commonalities in these contexts and thus do not offer a political theory to guide planning. Forester (1989), who provides the tables from which Table 6.1 is adapted, sets out the rationale for the concept of boundedness by saying that it is "an attempt to reformulate a comprehensive social and political theory of rationality. The task of any critical and social theory is to be able to distinguish the necessary and the unnecessary, and the ad hoc from the systematic constraints on social action so that appropriate responses will be possible" (pp. 215–216). The practical point raised by using this table to graphically represent the situations that planners confront, as opposed to views of politics assumed in other planning models, is "that expected and anticipated obstacles, opportunities, and thus practical strategies vary according to one's operative political theory" (Forester, 1989, p. 220).

Table 6.1 presents a template for how planners should read situations in terms of constraints to action resulting from particular relationships of power. Its four-cell design is created by crossing the source of the power relations (socially ad hoc versus socially systematic) and the relations among the interests of the legitimate actors in the planning process (consensual versus conflictual). In terms of the source of power relationships, some may be *socially systematic*—they are tied to existing organizational designs or political structures—and others may be relatively *ad hoc*—they derive from temporary organizational conditions or interpersonal relationships. Whereas the former represent ongoing and relatively unchanging relationships of power, the latter are transient because the capacity to act is limited to a particular planning situation. In terms of the table's second dimension, the people who have a legitimate stake in the program being planned may have interests that are largely the same (*consensual*) or different (*conflictual*). The distinction is important because when people with conflicting interests are involved in planning, those with the greatest amount of power will often exercise it in order to achieve their interests. If planners are to nurture a substantively democratic planning process in situations marked by conflicting interests and asymmetrical relationships of power, they need to use strategies that will give all legitimate actors an equivalent voice in constructing the program.

These political bounds on planners' actions must be anticipated because they are important determinants of what planners can do and should do in terms of nurturing a substantively democratic planning process. In order to plan responsibly, then, a planner must first recognize the situation for what it is (given the operative political theory) and then call on the appropriate strategy of response. Planners who misread the context will miss the chance to plan well. Using the metaphor from Chapter One, it is like crossing the crowded intersection with your eyes closed. Planners who treat systematic power relations as if they were ad hoc are likely to be ineffective; treating ad hoc constraints as if they were systematic is a form of paranoia (Forester, 1989). Likewise, planners who treat all situations as if they were consensual are likely to serve the interests of those who have the most power; whereas planners who treat all situations as if they were marked by conflicting interests are likely to be seen as suspicious and uncooperative. Of course, Table 6.1 cannot be a complete mapping of all situations that planners face in their practice; rather, it is a heuristic framework to focus planners' attention on what really matters as they seek a democratic planning process. Planners will find situations that lie along a continuum for both dimensions and do not fall neatly into one cell or another.

In the face of the four different situations laid out in Table 6.1, different strategies will seem appropriate for nurturing a substantively democratic planning process. Our position, which is that planners must condition their use of a particular strategy on the basis of the boundedness of the situation, is different from the models in the classical viewpoint. These models make strong assumptions about the planning situation and then offer a single best set of actions to undertake. In essence, these models assume there are no power relationships so the planner can follow the algorithms they prescribe. We suggest that for such situations, which Forester (1989, p. 54) calls "unbounded rationality," the optimal solutions of the classical models would work. In contrast, we assume that planners *always* encounter relationships of power that influence the judgments they make in constructing a program; the important task is to understand the nature of the political bounds. Moving from the highly idealized assumptions about planning situations inherent in the classical models, the four situations described in Table 6.1 run on a continuum such that the political bounds within which planners make their practical judgments become increasingly complex and structured (Forester, 1989).

Bounded Rationality 1: Individual Limits

Planners must first give up the ideals that underlie the classical models and begin to constrain the situations that arise in their everyday world. Planners work in a world of limited resources and time, as well as imperfect information. As Knox points out, "In contrast with idealized models of rational and goal-maximizing decision making, most able administrators 'satsificed' or muddled through by accepting courses of action that were merely satisfactory rather than the best" (1982, p. 61). Marti's situation in the OPD case is typical for adult education planners. She got an idea for a program based on her ongoing experience in working with people with disabilities. She sought and received permission to do the program for OPD before she involved anyone in the planning. From there, she had to plan the program with little assistance from support staff (limited resources), on a short time line (she had the idea in mid July and offered the program four months later), and without ever having done a program for this audience (limited information). She had no direct evidence about either the purpose or content for the program, nor had she developed a list of the potential audience members, yet she had about six weeks in which to put together and mail a brochure that would provide a detailed description of the program. Although the bounds she faced were relatively ad hoc and there appeared to be consensus among the interested parties, she quickly reached individual limits about what could be done to plan the program responsibly.

Her capacity to plan responsibly was constrained by particular sets of power relationships that meant that the optimal strategies of the classical models were simply not practical. The most appropriate planning strategy in these types of situations is to "satisfice" (Forester, 1989; March and Simon, 1958; Perrow, 1972), meaning to use satisfactory alternatives rather than optimal ones. Under these conditions of bounded rationality, Marti had to do what she could. She had to take shortcuts in deciding on the content for the program, for example, by deciding the topics to be covered rather than involving the potential audience in this judgment. Although the soundness of this judgment might be questioned (justifiably), she clearly read the context as constraining her capacity to involve the potential audience. In sum, by locating planning in the normal organizational world, what is practical and responsible shifts from an optimizing to a satisficing strategy (Forester, 1989).

Bounded Rationality 2: Social Differentiation

The situation can be further constrained if other people have a significant role in the planning process, even if their interests are consensual. Thus, the setting is differentiated in terms of a division of labor that is socially systematic. This is a more complex environment than that encountered by the planner in cell 1 because the planner must negotiate multiple interpretations of the emerging program. Further, not only are time and resources limited but they are unequally distributed among the people involved in planning; information is imperfect and is unequally distributed among the relevant parties (Forester, 1989). The setting for the pharmacy continuing education program could be seen as having these characteristics. The planners (Bob and Carl) were in a situation in which the division of labor required them to involve at least the content expert (Richard) and allowed them to involve representatives of the potential audience in constructing the program. Although everyone was fully cooperative in planning the program, the division of labor was clear about who could contribute what kinds of information in constructing the program. In other words, unlike Marti, Carl and Bob could not construct the program on their own because they were planning in a socially differentiated environment. They also had other organizations to deal with, such as the medical school campus of the university from which they felt compelled to draw faculty for the program.

In these kinds of situations, a satisficing strategy is not sufficient. Although some aspects of the planning may require a satisficing response, the more general strategy would be to network among all the parties that have information and authority to construct the program. This depends on having good working relationships with people within the organization as well as with people from outside agencies who might have a stake in the program. Networking means knowing who has what information relevant to the program, who has a legitimate stake in its outcome, and how to involve them in the relevant parts of the planning. The key here is forming and maintaining relationships with people who regularly contribute to the program planning in a particular setting. The network strategy works in these situations because of the similar interests among the people who need to be brought together to construct a program.

Bounded Rationality 3: Pluralist Conflict

The real world experienced by planners, however, is not usually so free of conflict. In many situations, planners face opposition as well as support from others who are potentially involved in planning a program. Planners routinely are confronted by conflicting claims of interests articulated by competing actors in the planning process (Forester, 1989). A good example can be seen in the ongoing interactions between Pete and George in the Phoenix Company case. This was a temporary relationship, having been formed for this particular program; in contrast was Pete's relationship with the president, which was rooted in the political structure of the organization and thus socially systematic. Pete and George had a clear conflict of interest about the purpose of the program, with George wanting to use the program to move the organization toward more participatory forms of management. George raised this point on several occasions and, in particular, pointed out that members of the audience ought to be involved in planning the program. However, Pete used his dominance in their relationship of power to protect his and the president's interests in keeping the management structure intact and to focus the program on better communication within the existing structure.

In these pluralist situations, the constraints become even more complex and difficult to work within in order to nurture a substantively democratic planning process. Not only is the setting socially differentiated but the different actors have competing interests and are willing to use asymmetrical relationships of power to further those interests. It is not a fully cooperative environment in which the problem is simply to identify the right people and involve them in constructing a program through various forms of consensual decision making. The planning process is characterized by different people using time, resources, and information to further their own interests in constructing the program. The central planning problem is no longer just to involve the appropriate people but whom to trust and what can be done to ensure that all relevant interests have an equivalent role in constructing the program.

In the face of pluralist conflict, networking is not a sufficient strategy, although it will be useful in certain respects. Rather, the overall strategy is one of bargaining among the competing interests. This happened in the Phoenix Company case when Pete went along with George's suggestion to use the "Desert Survival Exercise," although he and Joan were skeptical about its value. However, this was part of the overall bargaining they did with George to prevent him from pushing his interest in the purpose of the program; they allowed this format to become part of the program so that George would have some ownership in the program. Thus, short-term political compromise becomes the typical negotiating strategy, which can be a responsible approach as long as all affected interests are represented (Forester, 1989).

Bounded Rationality 4: Structural Legitimation

Settings of pluralist conflict may actually be less common than planners think. This account, which assumes that power relationships are distributed in an ad hoc manner, "may provide more consolation than guidance for it suggests not only that conflict is ubiquitous but also that there may be little pattern to the conflicts" (Forester, 1989, p. 58) that planners can expect. In the situations covered by cell 4, there are competing interests that are held by people engaged in asymmetrical relationships of power that are rooted in social and political organizational structures. Thus, people act within socially systematic and asymmetrical relationships of power when negotiating their interests in constructing an educational program. For example, to say that the interests of the president and the members of the audience for the Phoenix Company program were negotiated on equal terms is patently untrue. The president's claims about the purpose of the program, which was to improve communication, carried the day, with little regard as to whether this was the appropriate purpose from the audience's viewpoint.

In these situations, planning is likely to serve the interests of those who have the power. Planners are severely constrained, and unless they take clearly focused anticipatory action, their planning practices are likely to legitimate the interests associated with existing relationships of power. Under these conditions, bargaining is not a sufficient strategy for nurturing a substantively democratic planning process. Where the relationships of power are not only asymmetrical but rooted in social and political structures, bargaining may work in certain cases but will fail as a long-term strategy, because those who are dominant will ultimately see their interests through, as the president did at the Phoenix Company. Rather, planners need to anticipate how the relationships of power will affect the planning and counteract them in ways that give all affected interests an effective voice in constructing the program. Strategies that are most likely to address structural inequalities of power are "variants and kin of political and community-organizing strategies" (Forester, 1989, p. 62). Fundamentally, these strategies involve mobilizing groups of people to counter the effects of established interests. This may take a variety of forms, from providing information to potentially affected groups to active interventions to bring all affected groups into the process. Although many different strategies are needed to plan responsibly in the face of socially systematic power relationships, including satisficing, networking, and bargaining, such strategies can become more effective when planners are sensitive to the effects of such social power in the routine construction of educational programs.

The point of the chapter is simple and rooted in the common sense understandings of adult educators: different contexts require different planning strategies in order to nurture a substantively democratic planning process. Anyone who has ever planned educational programs recognizes this; Table 6.1 simply formalizes this idea according to a particular political theory.

Making the distinctions suggested in the table is no easy matter because contexts are usually difficult to read; thus, planners must have a theory upon which they can make a best guess regarding the nature of the power relationships facing them in practice.

However, planners' reading of the situation and the specific practical actions they take depend upon their understanding of how power relationships and interests are constituted and legitimated. Further, the ways that relationships of power structure planning situations are not fixed once and for all time but are constantly being reproduced or transformed and thus must be continually assessed. These difficulties do not mean planners should fail to take the context into account; as we argued earlier, planners cannot act at all, much less effectively, without reading the context. It does mean that reading the situation well is an essential part of responsible program planning. Finally, although the table suggests an overall strategy for each of the four contexts, planners need to draw on the entire repertoire of strategies as they face increasingly complex situations. The strategies should be seen as cumulative in that each one, while dominant in its own cell, can be called upon at the more complex levels as well.

SEVEN

Represent Interests Democratically

At the beginning of Chapter Six, we pointed out that adult educators regularly complain about the irrelevance of theory to their program-planning practice. The theories do not work, they say, because their practices are "very political," which is meant to end the conversation. If the ideas in the previous chapter are even half right, however, saying that "program planning is political" need not be the end of the conversation but rather "a fruitful beginning" (Forester, 1985, p. 218). As the cases in Chapters Three, Four, and Five amply demonstrate, program planners do not operate according to a script; rather, they are real people who must regularly negotiate between interests within a given set of power relationships in order to construct educational programs. In their daily work, then, planners are always faced with questions of what to do next and why. This calls for ethical thinking, by which we mean the capacity to think about questions of value, significance, and responsibility when deciding what action to take. We are not suggesting that an ethics of planning practice is necessary because it will produce the one right course of action (usually referred to as "the ethical thing to do") to take in a particular situation, for rarely is this the case. Rather, ethics is needed in planning so that planners have a sense of "what for" and not just "how to." Yet both are needed because if "ethical thinking is blind to the world of politics and

137

pragmatism, then ethics, it seems, asks us to be saints and martyrs, not planners" (Forester, 1990, p. 253).

Why People's Interests Matter in Planning Practice

In Chapter Six, we argued that the actual educational programs that planners construct are causally related to the exercise of their powers in accordance with their expressed and real interests. Chapters Three, Four, and Five showed the causal connection between the expressed and real interests of the people involved in planning and the purposes, content, audience, and format of the three programs. Of course, the interests did not plan the programs; the people did through the practical judgments they made in these four areas. These judgments, then, were neither random actions nor applications of a classical planning model but were causally connected to the interests of those who made the judgments. This view recognizes that program-planning practice is about people acting in the world in order to somehow make it different. They make it different by negotiating between concrete interests in the planning process. That educational programs are causally related to these interests is no superfluous claim, for we must ask: If programs did not depend on people's interests, what would they depend upon? Perhaps more important, if programs were not causally related to people's interests, why would it matter *which* educational programs were constructed? Educational programs matter primarily because they are a statement of how the world should be different; people's interests determine their important features.

If the actual form and content of programs depend upon the interests of those who construct them, a central ethical question involves whose interests are to be represented in program planning. For example, would the Phoenix Company's management education program have been different if the managers (the target audience) or the nonsupervisory employees of the company had been involved in constructing it? Pete clearly wanted to exclude these groups from the planning. Was this because they would have made a different statement about how the world should be in terms of the management practices at the company? The important point here is that the practical judgments about whose interests will be represented (and how they will be represented) in constructing a program are never a given. Planners have to continually make these choices in the situations described in Chapter Six and are constantly faced with questions not only of who can be involved, given the existing relationships of power, but whose interests are really at stake (and therefore should be represented) in the program to be constructed. These are essentially ethical questions that are addressed regularly by planners and thus require ethical judgments.

In this view, all planning practice takes one or another ethical stance because planners use it to try to construct programs that affect the world in a particular direction. As Knox points out, many people will be affected by an educational program; in addition to learners, "there are secondary outcomes to the agency, the parent organization, the general public, and even other providers of continuing education" (1982, p. 11). This is true whether it means changing the management practices of a company, providing pharmacists with the latest information about cardiovascular disease, or changing the attitudes and hiring practices of employers in regard to people with disabilities. That planners must operate from a particular ethical viewpoint should not be a startling revelation because why would anyone care about adult education if it did not intervene in the world in some way? Assuming that adult education (and therefore planning) is ethical, the central planning questions become in what ways the program will affect the world and who will make these judgments. To answer these questions in practice requires a specific vision or a belief system. As Griffith argues, "The professional practice of adult education rests upon a basic philosophy which calls for adult educators to have a coherent value position which gives direction to their work" (1978, p. 392).

A Vision for Planning Responsibly: Nurturing a Substantively Democratic Planning Process

If planning practice is an activity that is essentially ethical as opposed to strictly technical, planning theory must also be rooted in a particular set of ethics if it is to be instructive for the real judgments that planners routinely make. In Griffith's terms, such a theory must have an explicit value position that is not based solely on what works for those in power. Using the language developed in Chapter Six, we believe that adult educators have an ideal interest in nurturing a substantively democratic planning process. This belief makes our planning theory instructive for practice by providing the basis for its ethical dimension. While adult educators must, of necessity, always address actual relationships of power and the exercise of that power in terms of people's real and expressed interests, this ideal interest prevents the stress on politics from degenerating into a "disempowering relativism" (Hart, 1992, p. 197). In a very real sense, the ideal interest in democratizing planning is the vision of how educational programs should be constructed. Without this vision of responsible planning, adult educators would always be at the mercy of existing relationships of power and the educational programs they develop would be causally shaped by the interests of those with the most power.

If interests are chronically negotiated in any planning process, some ethical and strategic vision is needed to manage this process. Our vision of democratic planning means that all people who are affected should "be involved in the deliberation of what is important" (Apple, 1992, p. 11). As Frankel says of Dewey's democratic educational vision, "Democracy is a procedure for melding and balancing human interests. The process need not be conducted, and at its best is not conducted, without regard for truth and facts. . . . Its controlling purpose is collective action, not the accreditation of propositions as true" (1977, p. 20). Thus, a *democratizing planning process* means simply that real choices will be put before people about what collective action to take in constructing the curriculum, not that the people's action is true in some transcendental sense. By arguing for a democratizing process as the ethical and strategic principle for negotiating interests, we explicitly align ourselves with a particular intellectual and practical tradition in American education (Beyer and Apple, 1988). This stretches from Dewey's efforts to develop democratic forms of education to more recent attempts to reinterpret and extend this work in a way that recognizes the threats to democratic education posed by its relationship to the asymmetrical power relationships embedded in the social, cultural, political, and economic systems of American life (Apple, 1990; Collins, 1991; Giroux, 1983; West, 1989). It is impor-

tant, then, to say that planners have an ideal interest in a democratizing planning process and thereby articulate an ethical belief that
has been developed and validated by the evolving society in which
they live. If adult education is to have a positive and productive
relationship to the ongoing creation of the social, cultural, political, and economic systems of American life, it must abide by the
same ideal of the larger society. As Apple points out, "Democracy
is not a slogan to be called upon when the 'real business' of our
society is over, but a constitutive principle that must be integrated
into all of our daily lives" (1990, p. xvi).

   We can now tie together the themes of Chapters Six and
Seven by elaborating on the title of Chapter Six, "To Plan Responsibly, Be Political." We now expand that to read, "To Plan Responsibly, Be Political with a Vision." The vision is to nurture a
substantively democratic process in light of the asymmetrical relationships of power held by those people whose interests should be
negotiated in constructing the curriculum. Thus, in order to plan
programs responsibly, we need "pragmatics with vision" (Forester,
1993, p. 39). By saying that the vision is of a *substantively* democratic process, we mean to go beyond the simple techniques or formal structures of democracy (Forester, 1989; Giroux, 1983; Pusey,
1987), such as arranging learners in a circle and asking them what
they want to learn. Rather, planners have to recognize that people
act within a vast network of power relationships, some symmetrical
and some asymmetrical, as part of their participation in the larger
society and in the organizations within which programs are
planned. In this view, if planners treat all people equally under the
guise of equal opportunity, they help ensure that the interests of
those who have the most power will continue to be served (Forester,
1993). It is important to recognize, then, that the actual action taken
by a planner to nurture a substantively democratic process could be
different in different situations (as illustrated in Table 6.1). Con-
versely, the same action could nurture a democratizing process in
one situation while thwarting it in another.

   These points differentiate our planning theory from others
in adult education to which it bears a surface resemblance. For
example, many other theories also focus on involving learners in
the planning process. Knowles's theory of andragogy (1980), which

mentions the institutional context in only a general way and never broaches the subject of power relationships, provides a good point of comparison. We would argue that if Pete and Joan had used Knowles's andragogical planning principles for the management education program at the Phoenix Company, it is likely that a substantively democratic planning process would have resulted only if the power relationships of all involved were symmetrical. Of course, they were not, and this was precisely the problem Pete and Joan faced in the planning process. Even if they had explicitly involved the president, representative members of the vice president team, company managers, and other company employees in planning in equal ways, the program probably would have been the same in all important respects, given the enormous amount of power the president had in the situation. In order to nurture a substantively democratic planning process in this case, Pete and Joan would have had to base their actions on the recognition of this as a cell 4 situation (see Table 6.1) in order to articulate the interests of these other groups in constructing the program. As this case illustrates, planners need not only a vision but a vision that is linked with a political analysis because "good intentions when blind to the context of action can lead directly to bad results" (Forester, 1990, p. 253).

In this section, we have argued that planners have an ideal interest in a democratic planning practice, which is not justifiable simply by what works or does not work in a particular situation. Its rightness is not based solely on the realities of a given situation but rather on a belief that democratic planning is a form of social life that is just and morally legitimate. This ideal interest should be seen in contrast to the expressed and real interests of the people involved in planning, in that while real interests are structurally rooted, they are always constructed and reconstructed in actual planning situations and thus open to modification (Isaac, 1987). In sum, recognizing people's interests is a highly contingent process but one that is central to responsible planning.

Representing People's Interests in Planning Practice

If the actual educational programs that take place are causally related to the interests of the people who construct them, who is involved in planning (and in which judgments they are involved) obviously matter. While the strategic impulse of responsible planning should be that all people affected by the program have the right to participate in constructing it, knowing which people should be involved and how to create conditions for their substantive involvement is almost always an uncertain, ambiguous, and risk-taking activity. The reasons for this are many, not the least because, as described in Chapter Six, planners often must work in situations marked by asymmetrical power relationships that do not abide by this vision. However, this is further complicated when people have multiple and sometimes conflicting interests, some of which may be well known and explicit (expressed interests) and others of which may be so embedded in the ongoing social relationships that they are not conscious (real interests). Thus, no theory can unambiguously prescribe whether the actual people selected to construct a specific educational program are, in some transcendental sense, the right people. The planner must make a practical judgment in each and every situation based on pragmatics with vision.

In light of this point, we propose a heuristic device for recognizing who may have an interest in any educational program. We suggest that the interests of five categories of people are always represented when planning programs: learners, teachers, planners, institutional leadership, and the affected public (Boyle, 1981; Buskey, 1987; Griffith, 1978; Knox, 1982; Kowalski, 1988; Schwab, 1978). This list builds upon Knox's suggestion that "the three groups that should be included in decision-making are resource persons, potential participants, and administrators" (1982, p. 57). As happens in most planning situations and as was illustrated by the three cases, the same people can represent several categories. The scheme, however, rests on the assumption that each group has a potentially different set of interests in constructing the program. The important planning issues, then, are which people actually represent these interests, whether they are legitimate representatives, and whether they are the best representatives that could be secured in the situation.

Learners

Learners have an interest in constructing the program by virtue of their obvious role as the actual participants. Given the ubiquitous claim in most adult education program-planning models that learners must be involved, we need to point how our analysis reshapes this claim. Learners, too, are involved in complex sets of power relationships in the world, and these are an integral part of what they bring to any educational program; thus, there is no such thing as the generic learner, either in terms of power or of interests. Pete and Joan clearly recognized this at the Phoenix Company when, for example, they had to negotiate a way to limit the intrusion of the unequal relationships of power that actually existed among the different levels of company management during the experiential learning activities at the retreat. This was a potential problem because the company's management structure was organized around a hierarchical set of power relationships involving the vice president level, department managers, and supervisors. Yet the temporary learning environment at the retreat assumed that all participants would be treated equally. The planners were politically astute enough to know that if they had acted on the assumption of a generic learner, the unequal power relationships would likely have carried over into the program and could have hindered the achievement of their purpose. In sum, learners are people with particular interests who are engaged in networks of interpersonal, organizational, and societal power relationships that are an integral part of the planning process. By failing to recognize this, planners might be seen as unresponsive or, even worse, are likely to be ineffective.

Three central issues that are continually decided in planning are *who* actually represents the learner, *when* they are to be involved, and in *what* judgments they are involved. Although these issues may be separated for analytical purposes, they are continually played out in relation to each other as a program is constructed. First, the various potential representatives of the learners are all actual learners, some representative sample of actual learners or potential learners, or some other person who claims to represent the learners' interests. Second, learners could be involved in planning from the earliest stages. An important practical distinction can be made between the planning that occurs before the program and that which occurs during the program because the actual learners are always, by definition, present during the program. Finally, learners could also be involved in all the judgments from which a program is constructed, which we grouped into four areas—purpose, audience, content, and format.

In none of the three cases were the actual learners substantively involved in planning the program. The Phoenix Company presented the best opportunity for this because the audience was part of a closed system and was relatively small. Although the planners could have easily selected a representative group of actual learners (department managers), they explicitly excluded them because the planners believed they had enough experience at the company to represent the learners' interests and enough power to enact this belief. Thus, all the major judgments made before the program began—about the purpose, audience, content, and format—were made without the direct participation of the learners. During the program, the actual learners were directly involved in the construction of the content because of the emphasis on experiential techniques, such as the executive adventure that occurred on Thursday afternoon and the use of small group discussions and role playing throughout much of the Friday morning session. In a very real sense, the content of the program was constructed during those sessions. However, it is important not to lose sight of the fact that the planners made crucial judgments that framed this entire activity and thus limited the content that could have been developed. For example, the definition of the problem that the program was designed to address (the communication needs of upper management) was not likely to have been questioned within the learning formats chosen.

This case illustrates a common way of negotiating learners' interests: someone other than the learners (usually a teacher or a planner) represents their interests during the preprogram planning when many important judgments are made; then methods that draw on the learners' experience explicitly involve them in constructing the content during the program. It is significant that, by their presence and participation, the actual learners also have assented to the other judgments that were made in constructing the program, such as the purpose. Although this was a highly consensual form of negotiation in that no other features of the program changed while it was under way, this should not be confused with a lack of negotiation. It may have been that the program actually met the learners' expressed and real interests or that the learners did not believe they had sufficient power to renegotiate the curriculum to any significant extent at that time.

Teachers

Teachers' interests are often directly represented during the planning that occurs before the program and are always directly represented during the program. In using the term *teacher,* we recognize the common use made in adult education of a continuum that places more or less emphasis on the learners' experiences in constructing the curriculum. The terms usually used to represent the poles of the continuum are *subject matter expert* (for example, the faculty member Richard, in the pharmacy case) and *facilitator* (for example, the consultant George, in the Phoenix Company case). Regardless of the point on this continuum at which teachers are located, they always bring interests to planning. This occurred with Richard, who represented the real interests of the academic branch of the pharmacy profession (supporting the update model of continuing education), and with George, who represented his expressed interests in advancing participatory management practices.

The people who represent the teachers' interests may, by virtue of other roles they play, also represent other interests. Although the teachers and learners could be the same people (for example, in newly formed self-help groups), it is more likely that teachers are also the program planners, as Marti, Pete, and Richard were in the three cases, or members of the institutional leadership, as Pete was. By comparison, the faculty members (other than Richard, who was also a planner) of the pharmacy college and the OPD staff members were examples of people who represented only the teachers' interests. In the OPD case, faculty members were simply asked to deliver information about specific topics in which they had expertise; thus, they were actively involved in negotiating about the content of the program. In addition, by agreeing to participate as faculty, they assented (through consensus) to Marti's other judgments in regard to purpose, audience, and format.

The teachers in all three cases were involved in preprogram

planning and, by necessity, were involved in constructing the content and learning activities with the learners during the program. Teachers' interests are generally dominant from the preprogram planning through the program itself. This raises the most complicated program-planning issue to address: planners must delineate when teachers' power is a necessary feature of the division of labor in society (see cell 2 in Table 6.1) that vests them with appropriate authority for making judgments about content and when they have no socially necessary authority and thus should function as ordinary citizens. Of course, this becomes further complicated in actual planning situations when the same person (for example, Pete) represents the interests of the institutional leadership sponsoring the program, the planners, and the teachers. In this case, Pete was able to successfully accommodate his interests as a teacher in the program (and thus construct the program he wanted) because his dominant place in the power structure of the company allowed him to represent the institutional leadership (the president) and be the planner.

Planners

All educational programs have a planner, the person or persons responsible for negotiating the interests of people involved in its construction. Although this book is about the *planning* of educational programs, its focus is on the role of the *planner*. Planners are the people who are politically answerable for the program, often to many different constituencies. These various constituencies are engaged in complex relationships of power, which can make it difficult for the planners to reconcile (and sometimes even to recognize) the conflicting interests of those to whom they are politically answerable. Of course, planners are not neutral technicians who simply manage this process but are active members of the communities and organizations that construct the programs. Thus, they have a concrete place in the matrix of power, and their ability to negotiate between these interests is profoundly affected by that fact.

Because planners are not neutral in the negotiation between interests, it is clear that their expressed and real interests, as well as their own location in various power structures, must play important roles in the planning process. For example, Pete's real interest in strengthening the human resources function at the company led him to negotiate mainly with the president and selected vice presidents (entirely leaving out the executive vice president). In addition, his place in the company's power struucture enabled him to construct the program without the participation of intended learners (department managers) and members of the affected public (the majority of the company workers who would be directly affected by the changes these managers could make as a result of the program). To put this situation another way, the nonsupervisory workers (the affected public) could not have planned a program on communication patterns in the Phoenix Company without significant involvement by the institutional leadership. It is precisely because planners' interests *must* affect the planning process that their ideal interest of a substantively democratic process can materially affect how programs are constructed. The point is that how the program is constructed *will* be central to the exercise of planners' power; our argument is that democratizing planning should become an expressed interest of adult educators, thereby affecting their planning practice.

Unless planners have other roles as either teachers or learners, their negotiations between various factions is limited to the preprogram planning. As the three cases demonstrated, however, most major features of a program can be (though they need not be) fashioned before a program begins. As often happens, planners represent several other constituencies in the planning process by virtue of their multiple roles or because they choose to do so. For example, in addition to being the planner, Marti had interests as a teacher by virtue of her educational background in rehabilitation counseling and work experience related to people with disabilities. In addition, she chose to represent the interests of the potential learners for the program (personnel directors) and the public who might be affected by the program (people with disabilities). While her own disability might qualify her to serve as a legitimate representative of the affected public, having one person represent four different groups of people (planner, teacher, learners, public) certainly could have been a constraining factor in planning that program.

Institutional Leadership

When educational programs are planned within an institutional context (as they almost always are), the people in leadership roles have interests about which planners must negotiate in constructing the program. These people, such as Ann in the OPD case, have expressed and real interests that influence their exercise of power in providing leadership to the institution. They lead their institutions to act according to a certain mission and set of purposes, and to the extent that the educational programs planned in their institutions matter to the mission, planners should expect to negotiate about the same interests in constructing programs. This comes as no surprise to experienced planners who know that by acting as if these interests do not matter, they are "likely to fail miserably, to be misunderstood, to be seen as unresponsive, self-isolating, insensitive to the needs of others" (Forester, 1989, p. 7). All three cases showed that the planners involved the relevant members of the institutional leadership in key judgments about the purposes, audience, content, and format for the programs. Indeed, in both the OPD and the Phoenix Company programs, the director (Ann) and the president (Sam Jones), respectively, had to actually approve most major features of the programs.

Because program planners are almost always in asymmetrical (and nondominant) power relationships with the institutional leadership, their problem is not a matter of deciding whether to involve them (as it is with learners or the affected public) but how to involve people representing other interests in equivalent ways. Institutional leaders' interests are always negotiated about in constructing a program, whether directly (as in the OPD and the Phoenix Company cases) or indirectly (in the pharmacy continuing education case). By virtue of their role as institutional leaders, they represent the real economic, social, and political interests necessary to maintain or transform the ongoing life of the institution. Economic interests usually must be accounted for in any program-planning process. In the OPD case, Ann and Marti believed that any adult education activity offered by the institution needed to be self-supporting. The leaders also bring social interests to bear, such as Ann's interest in advocating social change for people with disabilities in all OPD activities, including its educational programs. As Ann said, any educational program had to represent a particular set of values consistent with those of OPD. Finally, these leaders' political interests were represented in all three cases. For example, the president of the Phoenix Company believed that the purpose of the educational program was to improve the patterns of organizational communication so that the company could operate more efficiently. In the pharmacy case, Bob represented the institutional leadership's interests (which were shared by Carl) in using the continuing education program to maintain the visibility and leadership of the college in the pharmacy profession.

In saying that educational programs are directly tied to institutional interests, it is important to stress that real people actually represent these interests in constructing the program. This is important in order to avoid an overly deterministic understanding of the role that this group of people and their interests play in constructing programs. First, as individuals, they are likely to have multiple interests that must be addressed, and where two or more conflict, one will likely take precedence. For example, the institutional interest in advocating social change for people with disabilities, which was represented by Ann, was in the end more important than her interest in using the program to leverage resources for OPD. Although she did insist that the program not lose money, she was prepared to go forward with the program, even if it was not likely to generate enough income to cover the staff time (primarily Marti's) devoted to the planning. Second, the interests of the institutional leadership are not some undifferentiated mass because almost always more than one person (and usually *many* more) could represent these interests. Thus, planners actually can have a relatively substantial amount of discretion in involving people with different interests in the planning process. This does not mean there will always be great differences in the interests of these people but that their expressed interests might be so different that it *would* matter who was actually involved. Pete's selective involvement of different vice presidents (based on who he believed was in the president's confidence) in the planning process is a good example of this practice. For example, Pete excluded Brad (the executive vice president) from the planning process but did include three vice presidents who had the president's ear.

The Affected Public

If educational programs are meant to have an effect on the world, it follows that the interests of those who might be directly affected by the outcomes of the program should be represented in constructing programs. Often, these members of the public are affected in terms of their relationship with the learners who participated in the program. A program is much like the rock that lands in a pond (the affected public) and forms concentric ripples. Some people are more or less directly affected by the knowledge the learners gained (or failed to gain) through the program. For instance, in the pharmacy case, one group of people who would be directly affected were those who use the services of pharmacists who might have attended the program (some of whom did, but most of whom did not). These people have an interest in pharmacists' being able to recognize cardiovascular disease and flag any contraindicated medications. Another affected group would be the pharmaceutical companies whose versions of drugs were used (or not used) to fill prescriptions for treatment of cardiovascular disease. A group that would be less directly affected would be, for example, the shareholders of the pharmaceutical companies, who stand to gain or lose income based on how well the company does in sales of drugs to treat cardiovascular disease. Our point here is not to exhaustively list all groups that might be affected. Rather, we wish to make clear that many people in addition to the actual learners are affected by an educational program and therefore have legitimate interests that are always represented by someone in constructing the curriculum.

If the interests of members of the affected public are always negotiated, the important practical question is which people actually represent those interests in the planning process. This is not an easy question because a generalized public interest usually does not exist. Rather, planners often are faced with the situation in which people who could represent the affected public have differing or even conflicting interests with regard to the educational program at hand. Marti faced this situation in planning "Meeting the Challenges of the Americans with Disabilities Act" for human resource directors responsible for hiring and training. Two groups that might be affected by this program were the people in leadership positions at the companies that employed the human resource directors and the people with disabilities who might be hired by these companies. Marti knew from her previous experience in the field that some companies were concerned that the law might require them to spend a great deal of money to make their physical plant and training programs accessible to people with disabilities. Thus, the interest of the companies might be a curriculum focused on what is minimally acceptable to comply with the law. In contrast, the interest of people with disabilities would be employment in positions for which they are qualified as long as their disability does not prevent them from carrying out the "essential aspects" of the job. Whichever interests were represented by the planners, the program would have been affected. In this case, Marti and the other faculty members represented the interests of the people with disabilities during planning. Thus, where there was a conflict among the various interests, the overriding interest of Marti and OPD in advocating social change caused her to favor the interests of people with disabilities. This does not mean that all employers have an interest in doing the least possible to comply with the law but that there are members of the affected public who have this interest and that an educational program could be constructed to achieve that purpose.

Although institutional leaders often directly represent their own interests, the interests of the affected public are more often represented by people who are also representing some other interest, such as the learner, teacher, planner, or institutional leadership. Planners may believe that these people can adequately represent the interests of the affected public. In the pharmacy case, Bob probably believed that the pharmacists representing the learners also knew what their customers needed and that the faculty, by being able to promote certain versions of drugs, represented the interests of the pharmaceutical companies. Whether these people actually represented these interests well is a rhetorical question for which we do not have an answer. The people most immediately affected in the Phoenix Company case, and who could have easily represented their own interests directly in the planning, were the other employees of the company. However, the planners took the position that they were running a business and that the interests of the top management were preeminent.

Linking Politics and Ethics in Planning Practice

To be truly practical, program-planning theories must be able to illuminate the ethical questions that planners routinely face in their everyday practice. There are two common misconceptions about how a planning theory can help an educator think ethically in practice. First, thinking ethically does not mean that a theory ought to attempt to specify formal rules that govern action because the ethical question of how planners should apply that rule in a specific situation will always remain (Forester, 1993). Nor does being ethically illuminating mean telling the planner to go out and do the right thing, which can make planners martyrs if following such maxims does not account for the various power relationships and interests. Our view is that a planning theory ought to locate practice in a world of influences that support or threaten the vision of good planning (Forester, 1993). Our theory is ethically illuminating, then, in the sense that it points out the threats (as well as the supports) that a planner can anticipate and proactively deal with to support a substantively democratic planning process.

Chapters Six and Seven must be read together because both the political and ethical views, the "how to" and the "what for," are needed for responsible program planning. We now restate the themes of the two chapters and condense them into three central points. The starting point is that educational programs are constructed by negotiating between the interests of the people who are involved in the planning process. In this chapter, we offer a heuristic way to categorize the groups of people who have potentially unique interests in the construction of any program. In our view, program planners negotiate between the interests of five groups whenever they develop a program: learners, teachers, planners (their own interests), the leadership of the institution in which the program is planned, and the affected public. Thus, the important practical question is not whether to negotiate between the interests of these groups. Rather, the issues that matter are which people actu-

ally represent the interests of the five groups, whether they are legitimate representatives, whether they are the best representatives in
the given situation, and how substantive their representation is.
Answers to these questions, we argue, must be guided by an approach we call *pragmatics with vision*. Our second point is that
some vision must guide planners in answering these questions. The
vision we propose is substantively democratic planning—all people
who are affected should be involved in the deliberation of what is
important about the program. However—and this is the third
point—planners must carry out this vision within a context of
power that either threatens or supports this vision.

EIGHT

Develop Skills
and Knowledge to
Negotiate Responsibly

In Chapter Two, we argue that program-planning practice is a social activity in which planners negotiate personal and organizational interests. In this third part of the book, we have built upon our definition of planning to offer an approach to planning programs for adults that is both politically astute and ethically sensitive. This chapter extends our approach to the arena of action by focusing on that most substantive and important planning activity, negotiating between and about interests.

Negotiating Interests: The Central
Activity of Planning Practice

Planning a program is not simply a matter of individual mastery and intuition. It is also a social activity in which people such as planners, teachers, learners, and institutional leaders seek to construct a program together. This "social construction" forms the core of planning by giving meaningful form to a program that is recognizable, coherent, and realizable by a variety of interested parties. In Pete and Joan's negotiations at the Phoenix Company with the president and with George, for example, they reviewed plans, criticized lists of objectives, and searched for alternative learning formats that promised better results. The design of the program (in terms of purpose, audience, content, and format) evolved not only in Pete's mind but more so in the shared program outlines that were reviewed and agreed upon by everyone involved in the planning. What evolves is not simply an abstract form but a socially constructed plan that emerges from a history of practical negotiations that link interested groups of people. This socially constructive notion of planning practice respects the intuitive aspects of creating programs and appreciates the thoroughly social and political character of the negotiation process through which any program becomes a reality (Forester, 1989).

In defining program-planning practice as a social activity in which people negotiate personal and organizational interests, we do not mean to diminish the importance of individual planners in that process. Rather, we wish to locate their actions as planners in a social world that both structures their action and is the means by which meaning is given to their actions. The central form of action in this social activity of planning, then, is to negotiate. By using this term we mean to emphasize its common usage as defined in *Webster's New World Dictionary* (1976): "to confer, bargain, or discuss with a view to reaching agreement with others." Planners work with people to construct programs, and their negotiations take a variety of forms, ranging from informal discussions to well-structured practical strategies and techniques. In the Phoenix Company case, Pete and Joan engaged in a continual stream of discussions that included formal meetings with Jones and with George for which agendas were written and during which decisions were made about all major aspects of the program. There were also many informal, spontaneous meetings and telephone conversations between Pete and Joan, between Pete and the other people at the company, such as the vice presidents, and between Joan and people outside the company, such as the consultants who conducted the executive adventure and the people in charge of the facility for the retreat. All these examples correspond to our definition of negotiation, which is to confer, bargain, or discuss with other people to arrive at the settlement of some matter. The point here is that people with interests plan programs, and specific adult education programs grow out of the actual negotiations among these people.

This understanding of negotiation allows for the fact that planning is carried out in some situations of widespread consensus and in some situations of conflict. Sometimes, the negotiations will occur amid conflicting interests, and the planner must mediate to arrive at an agreement or compromise. A typical example was Pete's discussion with George in the first planning meeting about whether to involve the department managers (who would be the majority of the participants in the program). George wanted to involve them in planning, while for a variety of reasons Pete did not. They had several exchanges about this and, in the end, decided not to further involve the managers in determining the program's purpose, content, and format. However, in some situations the interactions among people in the planning process is highly consensual, and the settlement of the matter under consideration is reached very smoothly. This is also a form of negotiation because people were involved in making a judgment about some aspect of the program. As we point out in Chapter Four, for example, the people involved in negotiating about the content of the pharmacy program, including the planner (Carl), teacher (Richard), institutional leader (Bob), and the potential learners, all had an abiding interest in the update model of continuing education. Thus, the two planning meetings that included these four groups began with the tacit agreement that the purpose of the program was to update practitioners about the latest research on cardiovascular disease and therapy. All the discussion among the people in the planning meetings supported this purpose; while the representatives of the learners, for example, could have challenged the topic or the update approach, they did not. Although there was no conflict about the purpose, the people involved in planning still had to agree on this aspect of the program. The important point to be taken from these two examples is that negotiation occurs when a course of action is chosen through the social interactions among people, regardless of whether they have similar or conflicting interests.

Planners may indeed negotiate in situations in which the people involved have similar interests, resulting in a highly consensual planning process. Even in those rare situations in which there is no conflict at any point in the planning process, however, planners are negotiating between people's interests in the context of power relationships. To clearly embed this characteristic of negotiation in our larger framework, we return to the distinction made in Chapter Six between power as an enduring set of relationships that gives planners (as well as others in the planning process) the capacity to act and the exercise of that power. In these terms, negotiating between interests is precisely where planners exercise their power. Thus, the source of planners' power and influence is rooted in their ability to manage and negotiate between the interests of those (potentially) involved in the educational process. As we have argued throughout this section of the book, planners' power and responsibility are linked as they negotiate about certain aspects of educational programs. Although planners' ability to negotiate between interests must, by definition, be done within the existing relationships of power, wide areas of discretion exist in terms of whose interests are represented and how they are represented in the planning process. We saw that the planners in the three cases had varying amounts of discretion in regard to who would represent the various interests in the planning process. The key issue for adult educators is how to exercise the discretion delegated to them by the existing power structure (that is, how they negotiate between interests) to plan any specific program.

Negotiation as Continually Reconstructing Power Relationships and Interests

As planners exercise their power in negotiating with interested groups, they construct the very visible outcome of an adult education program. Pete and Joan constructed a management education program, and Carl's planning practice constructed a pharmacy continuing education program, each of which was directly experienced by about seventy people. The primary visible outcomes of Marti's planning practice, because of the cancellation of the program, were the brochures announcing the event that were sent to about three hundred organizations. In this sense, these planners' practices, as is true for all program planners, constructed educational programs. If any educational program-planning model is to be helpful in practice, it must provide guidance on how to construct actual programs. Indeed, most of this book focuses on how to construct programs responsibly. Yet there is more to what is actually happening as planners negotiate between interests.

As Forester (1989) argues, "Every organizational interaction or practical communication (including the nonverbal) not only produces a result, it also reproduces, strengthening or weakening, the specific social working relations of those who interact" (p. 71). This characteristic of planning practice is necessary if planners are to take seriously the notion, presented in Chapters Six and Seven, that relationships of power and people's interests are not static but are continually negotiated. Our argument is that planners either maintain or transform the existing power relationships as well as people's expressed and real interests in negotiating to construct a program. That is, as people negotiate to construct a program, at the same time they reconstruct the power relationships and interests themselves. We are saying that this outcome of planning is universal and that it is important. In fact, most program planners recognize that reconstructing power relationships and interests is often as important an outcome as the program itself, and the adult educators in the three cases are no exception. Pete was not simply trying to design a program well but also to improve his standing (transform his power relationships) with the president and other vice presidents. Carl was not simply trying to offer pharmacists an update on the latest information about cardiovascular disease but also to maintain the relations of trust and respect of alumni and other practitioners for their state university. Marti was not only trying to change the attitudes of employers toward people with disabilities but also to establish OPD as an educational provider for local employers, thereby creating a new market for its services. These examples highlight the power relationships and interests that the planners explicitly recognized as wanting to influence. However, these planners negotiated in ways that had other important outcomes that they did not recognize. For example, Pete's judgment not to have the department managers directly negotiate for their interests in planning the program strengthened the existing power structure of the company in regard to who (namely, people in top management positions) could articulate the problems to be addressed by the human resource unit.

We can say that as planners negotiate interests, they also construct educational programs and reconstruct the power relationships and interests of those involved (or not involved) in the planning process (Forester, 1989). Planning practice always operates in these two dimensions, which are seamlessly connected, because planners cannot construct a program outside the social and political relationships among people involved in the planning. So even when planners are dealing with technical matters, such as which facility to use (see the Phoenix Company case), how to design the survey to determine which topics pique the interest of pharmacists (see the Pharmacy case), or how much money to charge participants to attend a program (see the OPD case), the judgments in these areas are structured by the social and political relationships among the people who make them. Thus, the decision to use an off-site facility for the management education program not only constructed a particular element of the program (its location) held at that site but also reconstructed (maintained) the political relationships of who *could* make that judgment at the Phoenix Company. This view suggests that while planners may be dealing at times with small matters as they negotiate between interests, their practice always raises the larger questions of the social and political legitimacy of their actions. As planners negotiate, they can expect to construct the visible educational program that will affect the world in a certain way and reconstruct, less visibly, power relationships and interests in regard to "knowledge (who knows what), consent (who exercises power and who obeys), trust (who cooperates with whom), and the formulation of problems (who focuses on and neglects which problems)" (Forester, 1989, p. 80).

In sum, planning practice as embodied in the central activity of negotiating interests is as much an action in the world as the educational program that is constructed; while the impact on power relationships and interests is often less visible, it is no less important. It is perhaps most useful to think of the reconstruction of power and interests in historical terms. Pete and Joan clearly thought about the effect of their planning practices on the management education program in these terms. They realized that any future planning would be done against the backdrop of the power relationships and interests among the people in the company as reconstructed in negotiations for the 1992 program. Previous research (Beder, 1978; Cervero, 1984), as well as our own experience, tells us that Pete and Joan are not unique in understanding that their planning practices have two sets of outcomes. It should not be surprising that most effective planners recognize the dual level at which they are operating, because they live and must practice in a historically developing world. They certainly know that any effort to negotiate between interests without regard to the history of their organization would significantly increase the risk of failure. Because of this sensitivity to institutional history, planners are concerned with how they can reconstruct, either by maintaining or transforming, the relevant power relationships and interests in order to carry out their vision of good planning. If the central activity of program planning is negotiating interests and this activity both constructs educational programs and reconstructs power relationships and interests, the next questions are what planners must know and do to carry out the vision of planning responsibly.

What Planners Must Know in
Order to Negotiate Responsibly

Adult educators obviously approach each program-planning activity with some knowledge and skill that directly influences how they act and, therefore, how the important features of any program are constructed. If this is true, we must be able to specify what adult educators should know or learn to do as they face any new program-planning opportunity. As we point out in Chapter Two, we are fortunate to have nearly fifty years of scholarship and even more years of practical planning activity on which to draw in answering this question. This is a crucial point because it undergirds the entire discussion in this section: planners already have a vast repertoire of technical, political, and ethical knowledge and skill with which to negotiate responsibly. Therefore, the problem for the field of adult education is not necessarily to invent any new strategies but to develop a different way of looking at planners' existing knowledge and skill. The view we offer in this book is of negotiation as planners' central activity.

The image of negotiating interests requires us to reconfigure the essential knowledge and skill that planners need. We do this by first explaining why the classical planning model (with its series of planning steps) must be abandoned as the organizing framework for

this knowledge and skill. Boyle, one of the most articulate propo-
nents of the classical viewpoint, puts it most directly in explaining
the use of planning models in practice: "Program development is
essentially the art of designing and implementing a course of action
to achieve an effective educational program. This simple definition
implies that the continuing educator is involved in reaching decisions through the implementation of a rational or developmental
model. However, it should be recognized that a completely rational
model is rarely, if ever, achieved *in the practical world of planning
with people*" [emphasis added] (1981, p. 42). To paraphrase Boyle,
if a model does not account for the central role that people play in
planning practice, it does not fit the realities of program planning.
This leads us to ask, If it is so obvious to all adult educators that
the central dynamic of planning is that programs are planned with
people, why not make this model the basis of planning theories? By
moving people to the center of our framework, we necessarily draw
attention to the knowledge and skill that planners need to act responsibly in the face of power relationships and complex and competing arrays of people's interests. The knowledge and skill needed
in this vision of planning simply cannot be circumscribed by the
boundaries of the classical planning models, because these models
do not deal directly with the central dynamic of power and planning practice, either in terms of the construction of educational
programs or the reconstruction of social and political relationships.

As the people responsible for negotiating about interests,
planners need three kinds of knowledge and skill for constructing
adult education programs (Forester, 1989; Habermas, 1971). They
need technical knowledge and skill about how to construct educational programs effectively. Depending on the specific context in
which the adult educator is working, this can include how to design
surveys and evaluation instruments, organize and manage group
learning activities, select and train instructors, write budgets, and
market and publicize programs to the potential audience. While
these skills are necessary at various points in the planning, they are
not sufficient for negotiating responsibly. Planners also need political knowledge and skill in order to be able to get things done
with the people in the social and organizational contexts in which
they work. For instance, they need to be able to work with other

people and develop their trust and respect, understand the formal and informal power structure of the organization, and know which strategies will and will not work in their setting. However, technical and political knowledge alone will not tell planners what is truly at stake as they construct programs. Adult educators also need ethical knowledge in terms of both the educational programs that are constructed as well as the sociopolitical relationships that are reconstructed. They must focus knowledge and skill on the importance of nurturing a substantively democratic planning process in the face of a power structure that either threatens or supports this vision of responsible planning. Planners must be aware of their own interests and which risks can and must be taken to represent all relevant interests in the planning process.

Ethical Knowledge and Skill

As social beings with interests and values, planners do care about and are committed to bringing about a certain kind of world through their efforts. Planners are always affecting the world in a particular direction and closing off other directions. This is not news to anyone involved in adult education. A good example is that the content and objectives for all three programs discussed in the book were not predetermined; the planners for any of the programs could have easily developed different objectives that would have affected people differently. No less an authority than Ralph Tyler (1949) speaks to this point about the formative character of curriculum planning: "It is certainly true that in the final analysis objectives are a matter of choice, and they must therefore be considered value judgments of those responsible for the school" (p. 4). In other words, after all the information is collected about what might be taught in an educational program, the values of those who are responsible for the program determine what is actually taught. Tyler's statement illustrates two fundamental reasons that planners' ethical knowledge and skill are essential. First, their own interests and values are clearly going to affect any program they are involved in planning. We saw numerous examples of this throughout the three cases. In addition, the planner is the person who negotiates between the interests of "those responsible" for the educational program. Depending on their own interests and values, planners would have different answers about who is responsible for the program. For example, do those responsible include the teacher, the learner, the institutional leadership, and the affected public? When should the people representing these interests be brought into the planning process? Planners' ethical knowledge and skill in regard to these questions profoundly affect the shape of the educational program that is constructed.

Planners must be ethically sensitive to the fundamental link between the people whose interests are represented and the central features of the program that is constructed, as well as the political relationships that are reconstructed. Ultimately, planners have to take a stand about who will represent which interests in making the judgments about the purposes, audience, content, and format of the program. Because planners always have to decide who will represent which interests, they need to attend to the ways in which power relationships among people strengthen certain interests and silence others. Thus, a necessary part of planners' ethical knowledge is awareness of the commitment to a substantively democratic planning process of the people involved. It is probably wise to expect less, rather than more, of a commitment to this ethic of planning. Planners need to have their antennae up in order to gauge people's commitments to democratic planning, because there will almost always be pockets of support even where those with the most power reject it. Part of planners' ethical skill is knowing how to read these commitments and use them to build a democratic planning process.

Finally, planners must be clear in their own hearts and minds about their own expressed and real interests with regard to constructing any educational program. We have argued that adult educators have an ideal interest in democratic planning, because democratic social relationships form American society. Just as these forms of democratic relationships are threatened in other sectors of society, so too are they not always valued in the educational process. Yet while adult educators must always take into account the historically developing power structure within which they must act, they can only do so with some ethical vision of the forms of relationships upon which they wish to base the planning. For example, Boyle's (1981) rationale for the "involvement of people in program development" concludes with the following ethical principle, with which we only partially agree: "the design of the process of involvement should be based upon the program situation rather than on the soundness of the idea of involvement" (p. 106). While we certainly agree with Boyle's point—that deciding who should be involved in planning is a practical matter that must be made within the constraints of a particular context—he explicitly argues that these constraints are the only arbiter of who should be involved. In our view, this is a recipe for allowing the interests of those with the most power to determine the form and content of the program while strengthening their own power.

Having an ethical belief that all people affected by an educational program should be involved in constructing it usually means that planners will run some risk in the planning process. These risks might show up in the educational program itself, perhaps affecting its success, or in the political arena, perhaps threatening the adult educator's power within the organization. In certain situations, for example, people representing the interests of institutional leadership (as in the Phoenix Company) may believe their interests are most important. As Kowalski observes, "Private industry, in particular, is not overly prone to involve large numbers of employees in planning activities" (1988, p. 104). In other situations, potential learners may be reluctant to become a part of the planning process. While assessing the risks of involving various groups, responsible planners must ultimately know the strength of their own belief in a substantively democratic planning process. Along with this, they must have the knowledge and skills necessary to take these risks in a politically astute and technically sound manner.

Political Knowledge and Skill

The ethical knowledge used by adult educators is not always an explicit part of their planning repertoire; the knowledge and skill they need to deal with political realities typically holds center stage. Like any other human activity, planners "need to be able to work with others, to develop trust, to locate opposition and support, to be sensitive to timing, and to know the informal 'ropes' as well as the formal organizational chart" (Forester, 1989, p. 80). Without this knowledge, planning simply could not occur in anything resembling a responsible fashion, because the planner would be overwhelmed by the politics of the situation. The planner needs organizational savvy and diplomatic skills to recognize which people can and must represent which interests in planning to give the program credibility with its various constituencies. Knox (1982) supports this by arguing that "in the best practice, the planning process is very interactive and success depends on effective interpersonal relations. Such success begins with getting along with people and proceeds to the mastery of procedures for shared decision-making" (p. 66).

If for no other reason than that they need the knowledge to survive, planners often have a tremendously rich reservoir of political knowledge and skill (Dominick, 1990; Dougherty, 1990). Unfortunately, the literature upon which adult educators can draw is underdeveloped and does not do justice to their sophistication. As Brookfield, one of the major theorists in adult education, confesses, "The chief element missing from my own professional preparation as an adult educator was the awareness that adult education programs were created in political situations, were open to alteration as a result of political decisions, and were dependent on a favorable political climate for their continuance" (1986, p. 228). There are increasing efforts to identify political knowledge and skill as a necessary component of planners' repertoires of action (see Simerly and Associates, 1987, and Sork, 1991, as examples). As two authors in the Sork anthology found in a study of factors associated with successful adult education programs, planners need to "be concerned with creating and maintaining positive relationships [which] calls for the planner to exhibit negotiation and networking skills" (Lewis and Dunlop, 1991, p. 26).

Several authors have urged planners to analyze the planning context as a first step in constructing any program (Boyle, 1981; Buskey, 1987; Caffarella, 1988; Knox, 1979; Kowalski, 1988). Sork and Caffarella's work (1989) illustrates this by advising planners to identify the internal and external forces that will affect their planning. Some internal forces they describe are the history and tradition of the organization, the current structures that govern the flow of communication and authority, the mission of the organization, and the resource limits. Some authors have gonè even further, by describing specific strategies that can be used to negotiate between interests in a politically astute manner (see Simerly and Associates, 1987, for a good example). Some writers have even directed our attention to the reconstructive aspects of planning by pointing out that developing a specific program has long-term consequences for any organization. As Buskey (1987) points out, "The programs planned and executed this year provide the programming and financial base for next year and the years that follow" (p. 103). Buskey also notes, however, that most adult educators, as well as the literature in the field, tend to conceive of program planning as a short-term activity, thereby missing its significance for the longer-term strategic needs of the organization.

Even if the program-planning literature were to capture and make explicit the sophisticated political knowledge that practitioners use in practice, we need still more in order to negotiate between interests responsibly. Planners must recognize the ways in which the contexts in which they plan are socially and politically constructed and that specific political strategies will work only if the situation is assessed correctly. To this end, Table 6.1 offered an explicit theory of the political boundedness of planning, thus giving planners a strategy for reading and acting within the different relationships of power present in all situations. The key value of this analysis is that it situates power at the center of planning practice and helps planners become politically skilled at anticipating how power in an organization will affect the negotiation between interests. In this way, planners can act in an anticipatory, as opposed to reactive, fashion. For example, by anticipating how political pressures are likely to shape planning judgments, planners can compensate for them. By anticipating the interests and commitments of the various groups affected, planners can build the political support necessary to allow these groups substantive access to the planning process. To the extent that planners develop these anticipatory skills, they enrich their efforts to negotiate in ways that nurture substantively democratic planning.

Technical Knowledge and Skill

Even with excellent motives, planners will not get far without knowing, for example, how to construct a valid survey, organize and manage a planning meeting, develop an appropriate mailing list and get the publicity out on time, be aware of the variety of instructional techniques that can be used, find and select good teachers, select facilities appropriate to the instructional format, and prepare a credible budget. Planners need to know the features of any program that must be negotiated (such as purpose, content, audience, and format), when they must be negotiated, and what kinds of information will be needed to make responsible judgments in these areas. Without these skills, or access to them through other people on staff, planners are likely to be seen as well-meaning people with nothing to offer. Indeed, much of the program-planning literature is addressed to the wide range of technical knowledge and skills planners should have.

At the same time, Brookfield (1986) has criticized the literature "for its view of planning as an applied skill which exists somehow independently of political and moral considerations" (p. 231). While this characterization may be true of the literature (and in many cases it is a fair description), adult education planners can hardly afford such a sterile view of their work. Technical knowledge and skill are *always* used in a political context; in other words, planners' technical knowledge can make a difference in how a program is constructed, not because it is technical but because the institutional roles of planners who use these skills are politically legitimate. For example, Bob and Carl designed a survey that asked pharmacists from around the state what topics they would be interested in for the 1992 annual seminar. Even assuming that this was a technically sound survey, this was not why the data generated from the survey were used to determine a topic for the seminar. Rather, the data were used because the people who needed the information (Bob and Carl) were in positions of authority such that they could use the data. Thus, in all cases, planners' ability to make technical judgments is derived from their political position: "Once reported or uttered, even the most technical judgment becomes an integral part of the political world; it becomes inescapably political, seeking legitimacy by appealing to the consent of those concerned with the merits of the case" (Forester, 1989, p. 72). This does not deny the importance of planners' technical knowledge; rather, it locates it in the world in which planners actually use it.

While technical skill and knowledge must be refined in practice, the literature in adult education program planning covers many important aspects of the repertoire that planners need. Indeed, we cannot do justice to this vast literature except to point out some major signposts. For those interested in constructing programs using a certain format, the literature offers specific guidance about planning, such as workshops (Sork, 1984) and conferences (Ilsley, 1985; Nadler and Nadler, 1987). Some authors make the case that constructing programs is greatly affected by type of institution and so offer specific guidance about planning programs, for example, in higher education institutions (Freedman, 1987; Gessner, 1987) and business and industry settings (Nadler, 1982). Finally, there are many useful overviews of the technical information planners need in specific areas such as marketing (Beder, 1986; Simerly and Associates, 1989), involving learners in planning (Rosenblum, 1985), and using experiential techniques (Lewis, 1986).

Those seeking comprehensive and integrated views of the technical information planners need will find Knox (1986), Boyle (1981), Kowalski (1988), Caffarella (1988), and Houle (1972), among others, quite helpful. Of particular significance is that the authors explain the judgments that planners will have to make in constructing adult education programs. In Chapters Three, Four, and Five, we used one of these formulations, namely, that the most important areas in which planners made judgments were the purpose, audience, content, and format for the three programs. Although the areas identified as important vary, Sork and Caffarella (1989) have synthesized the literature in six basic elements: analyzing the planning context and client system, justifying and focusing planning efforts (primarily on the basis of a needs assessment), developing program objectives at some level of generality, formulating an instructional plan (including selecting and ordering content, designing the instructional process, selecting resources, and determining evaluation procedures), formulating an administrative plan (including assuring participation and program financing), and designing a program evaluation plan (starting with achievement of the program objectives). Planners who are aware of the areas in which they will have to negotiate, whether these six or some other configuration, can better anticipate the kinds of information that will be needed, who will need to be involved in the planning process, and when and how best to involve other people in making the decisions.

Planners' Roles in Practice

What are the implications for planners' roles when negotiating is seen as the central activity of their practice, one that both constructs educational programs and reconstructs political relationships? As we stated in Chapter Two, the literature has paid so much attention to the technical information and skills that planners need that many people believe, even in the face of daily experience that teaches them otherwise, that their primary role is that of a technical consultant, artfully managing the planning process with a repertoire of strategies and techniques. Although this is clearly one role that planners play, it sells the complexity of their practice far short. For, as planners negotiate interests, they also play the role of social activist (as they deal with ethical questions) and political organizer (as they deal with questions of power). Although planners routinely put into practice a wide range of ethical and political knowledge and skill in constructing adult education programs, the planning literature has not developed an understanding of the knowledge necessary in these two areas in anything approaching the sophistication exhibited for technical knowledge. Our view calls for an expanded definition of planners' roles so that they negotiate in an ethically sensitive, politically astute, and technically sound manner.

NINE

Understand Planning
as a Social Practice

Throughout this book we argue that planners negotiate interests to construct the world in which they live. As the cases and our arguments show, educational programs for adults emerge from the personal and organizational interests of the people involved in planning. Simply put, planning is world making, which is why it matters and why planners should care about doing it better. In putting forth this claim, we believe that our analysis offers a new theoretical understanding of the nature of planning practice. Our central thesis in this respect is that planning is a social practice, not a scientific one. As we have shown, theoretical depictions of planning practice as various permutations of the classical viewpoint are epistemologically inaccurate and morally and politically naive. And while the naturalistic and critical viewpoints have provided valuable insights, they too are unable to depict accurately how planners actually plan in the real world, for none of the traditional viewpoints can adequately account for the structured yet contingent nature of planning. Earlier chapters present a view of planning practice as ethically, politically, and structurally sensitive practical human action. In this chapter, we seek a theoretical understanding of why those accounts make sense. Thus, this chapter addresses why we had to write this book—the failure of planning theory to fully account for planning practice. Our central concern, then, lies in examining the intellectual traditions upon which we have drawn to portray planning as a social practice, one squarely within a context of people acting purposefully in structured relationships of interests and power.

We examine four broad themes in this chapter. First, we examine the traditional theoretical orientation of the field of adult education. This is the tradition that has expressed a rather unwavering faith in science as a source of solutions to practice problems, a faith that has led directly to a theoretical insistence upon comprehensive, scientific rationality. This tradition has sought to improve practice through the application of the scientific method but has largely been inadequate because of its inability to account for the complexities of actual practice. Second, we sketch the emerging tradition of the practical as a more accurate portrayal of the daily activities of planners and show how such a view replaces the traditional scientific-rational understandings of adult education practice. For us, practice cannot be portrayed in ideal scientific or simple technical terms. Such portrayals sell practice short by failing to account in any adequate way for the central involvement of people, interests, and power in planning practice. Yet even in the recent attempts upon which we are drawing (Bright, 1985; Cervero, 1989; Schön, 1983; Usher and Bryant, 1989; Usher, 1991), which attempt to resituate adult education as a practical rather than scientific endeavor, still missing is an adequate understanding of how planners are able to act purposefully in structured yet contingent social settings of interests and relationships of power.

In regard to this concern, we draw upon theoretical accounts (Giddens, 1979, 1984; Isaac, 1987; Lave, 1988) that fundamentally situate planners' action in the real world of enabling and constraining conditions. Here we expand the claim, introduced in Part Three, that we must have a better understanding of practice as a social endeavor. This requires locating practice in an adequate theory of human action, one emphasizing the essential recursiveness of daily life, which Giddens (1979) has described as the dialectical interdependence of human action and sociocultural context. Our purpose is to contribute to the emerging reconstitution of the theoretical depiction of adult education as practical, political, and ethical, rather than scientific. We do so in a way that begins to meet Giddens's challenge "to overcome traditional dualisms of subject and object" (1979, p. 120) in social analysis: that is, to integrate knowledgeable social actors (agents) in socially structured settings (structure). In sum, our goal is to elaborate a theoretical basis for understanding practice as human action within structured social contexts (Forester, 1990; Isaac, 1987). Such an integrated view of knowledgeable, purposeful planners acting contingently within relationships of power seriously challenges the traditional scientific basis for improving the practice of planning. Therefore, we conclude with a discussion of a reconstituted theory-and-practice relationship in adult education, one in which theory helps illustrate the very real and daily ethical and political, as well as practical, challenges of planning practice. Here we introduce a broadened view of theory and its relationship to practice, one that is empirically grounded, practically appropriate, and ethically illuminating (Bernstein, 1976; Forester, 1993; Habermas, 1971). Without such a basis, we cannot meaningfully talk about improving practice.

Comprehensive Rationality: Science and Planning Practice in Adult Education

A central ideological structure on which the modern practice of adult education has been predicated (Knowles, 1980) is a belief in the ability of science to solve educational problems. In this model, practice is improved by using the method of science as a model for rational human action (Schön, 1983). We believe this assumption has dominated the "theory-to-practice" relationship in adult education. This set of beliefs about the instrumental value of science to the practice of adult education has become so orthodox as to be almost unquestionable. Perhaps Long stated it best when he claimed that the "scientific method is one of the most promising tools available . . . to increase the accumulation of tested and verified truth" (1980, p. 7). Long's view echoes the earliest days of the professionalization movement in adult education (Beals, 1936; Houle, 1948). This belief in science has been central to the field's attempts to understand the practice of program planning.

Consequently, it is important to sketch the traditional theory-to-practice relationship in order to see how this book's arguments are fundamentally different. In the conventional model, borrowed largely from the natural sciences, practice is a process of applying theoretical principles developed from scientific research: "professional activity consists in instrumental problem solving made rigorous by the application of scientific theory and technique" (Schön, 1983, p. 21). In this model, research and theory are privileged because it is their task to produce knowledge that practitioners can use. Such research-based, scientific knowledge seeks to report on the world as it is, independent of human perception. Thus, theory is used to organize the world so that practitioners can act more reasonably in it, that is, in ways less susceptible to situational vagaries and perceptual idiosyncrasies. As Schmidt and Svenson argued in 1960, there is "the continuing need for experimentation and research so that adult educators make crucial decisions on the basis of dependable evidence, rather than on intuition and limited experience" (p. 94). Comprehensive, rational action, then, is predicated on the ability of science to learn how the world really works and derive causal explanations of why it works. This is necessary so that practitioners can have "predictive" knowledge of their circumstances and thereby can better control the conditions of their practice (Carr and Kemmis, 1986; Habermas, 1971; Schön, 1983; Usher and Bryant, 1989). In other words, the scientific model portrays practice as consisting of sets of predictable problems, the solutions to which, revealed by scientific research, are largely technical in nature: "practice is equated with technique and thereby relegated to an instrumental and subordinate position in relation to theory" (Usher and Bryant, 1989, pp. 78-79). Theory—developed through scientific research—is thus above practice in the hierarchy and therefore forms it.

Emanating from this tradition is a view of human rationality as comprehensive and scientific. Comprehensive rationality proposes a means-ends logic that features a given goal to be met and a process whereby all consequences possible can be factored into decision making. Mehan describes comprehensive rationality as requiring "the consideration of all possible alternatives, an assessment of probability of each one, and an evaluation of each set of consequences for all relevant goals" (1984, p. 46). Forester (1989, p. 49) describes this model as the ideal "rational-comprehensive" position, which assumes a well-defined problem, a full array of alternative solutions, total information about all consequences, full awareness of the intentions of all interested parties, and unlimited time to analyze consequences. First proposed by Descartes' *Discourse on Method* (1637), this model of rationality permeates the Western world's version of how humans solve problems and is central to both natural and social science traditions. The true essence of comprehensive rationality is, in fact, an argument for a highly decontextualized procedure of inquiry, commonly known as the *scientific method.* That is, given the comprehensive rationality of the scientific method, the solution to any problem can be determined and then applied to practice.

This model of rationality is well documented in adult education planning theory, which we have referred to as the *classical view* and is perhaps best illustrated in Tyler's curriculum planning steps (1949). As we argued in Chapter Two, scientific or comprehensive rationalism provides the logic and assumptions underlying nearly all the adult education planning literature reported by Sork and Buskey (1986). This is not to say, however, that the model is not under some suspicion, as some have indicated (Brookfield, 1986; Houle, 1972). But it is such a dominant framework for understanding practice that in their comprehensive review of adult education planning literature, Sork and Caffarella (1989), while expressing concern about its utility, still invoke the classical viewpoint—with its hierarchical theory-to-practice relationship—as the best way to conduct planning practice. Yet even after privileging the logic of the steps of the classical viewpoint as the preferred sequence, Sork and Caffarella acknowledge that there are "shortcomings in the planning literature that need to be addressed" (1989, p. 243); they suspect the shortcomings derive from the exigencies of day-to-day practice. Although Sork and Caffarella point to emerging notions of "theory-in-practice" (Schön, 1983), their clear reference to the theory-practice "gap" (p. 243) assumes the traditional response to this problem, which is to seek more scientific research in order to improve practice. This represents the concern typically expressed about adult education, its lack of a theoretical and research-derived information base to guide practice. We believe this concern has driven the field since the 1930s (Beals, 1936; Wilson, 1992). For example, Houle laments the lack of "proper objective evidence on which generalizations might be based" (1948, p. 276). He believed this continuing concern owed to a lack of professionalization in the field because "many of the fundamental principles which underlie successful theory and practice have yet to be discovered" (1960, p. 128). Indeed, Rubenson (1982) argued that the field of North American adult education was not only "undertheorized," it was largely, in fact, "atheoretical," a concern that Long recently echoed in his 1991 description of the field's information base as "nonaccumulative" and "atheoretical." The characteristic concerns, then, are that the field needs more scientific research to generate better theory in order to improve the "scientific" practice of adult education.

Although systematic inquiry is important, our argument is that the proposals for understanding the nature of practice and its ends as the application of comprehensive scientific rationality fundamentally misconstrue the essential nature of planning. Our point is that the reason a comprehensive rational view cannot provide an adequate basis for practice is the direct result of its epistemological and ontological limitations for understanding an actual planner's actions in the real world. In other words, the classical, as well as the naturalistic and critical viewpoints, have been unable to produce a theoretical depiction of the purposeful planner in a structured social world, that is, to meet Giddens's challenge of linking agency and structure. As we argue in Chapter Two and reiterate here, the classical view predicates program planning on a view of planners' actions as unencumbered, decontextualized, and comprehensively rational. But such pleas for scientific rationality, like that laid out by the classical view, fail fundamentally to understand how humans act in the real world. This claim is one of the central concerns in the arguments in regard to the postempiricist philosophy of science and the protracted debates regarding the efficacy of Western scientific rationalism; our intent is not to engage in that discussion here, for it is well portrayed elsewhere (Bernstein, 1976; Bright, 1989; Carr and Kemmis, 1986; Habermas, 1971; Isaac, 1987; Usher and Bryant, 1989). We need only to envoke that conversation in order to argue that the conventional model of scientifically derived, rational human action is severely limited in understanding how planners construct programs. As counterpoint to the stipulations of a science-based theory of human action, we turn to a discussion of the practical in order to argue for an alternative theory-and-practice relationship in adult education and to conceptualize the essential "situatedness" of planning practice.

Using Practical Reasoning in Planning Practice

As we discuss in Chapters Two and Six, "comprehensive" notions of rationality do not well suit the everyday world of planning practice. In the daily world of planning, planners can rarely afford the luxury of comprehensive rationality, for the action orientation of everyday planning requires sensible and satisfactory solutions rather than comprehensive or hypothetical and deductive ones (Rogoff, 1984). This is not to say that planners do not act rationally; indeed, a good portion of this book is concerned with demonstrating that planners' actions are rational. But it is to say that comprehensive notions of scientific rationality as underlying planning theory fundamentally fail to understand how planners act in the real world, for this mode of rationality lacks the crucial ethical, political, and structural dimensions that make sense of planners' actions in a context of interests and power. Thus, the challenge in understanding practice is also the challenge of solving this essential problem in planning theory. In order to begin to reconceptualize the practice-and-theory relationship in adult education, we build on the pragmatic tradition. This position understands the world of planning as socially situated and indeterminate and, in turn, depicts planners as action oriented rather than comprehensively rational. In doing so, we describe the (re)emerging tradition of practical reasoning as a way of understanding the rationality of planners' actions and then discuss some of its limitations in order to show how this book attempts to link agency and structure.

Planners' Actions in Context

In order to develop an understanding of planning as situated in a context and planners' actions as practical, we first turn to Peirce and Dewey's pragmatic development of it in the progressive view of education. Theirs is a view of individual action as inherently social by nature; Peirce always emphasized "the social character of the individual. The very nature of the individual is determined by his [sic] forms of participation in community life" (Bernstein, 1971, p. 190). That is, we cannot reasonably conceive of human action without considering its location in and derivation from its social context. But this extremely significant awareness is lost in the construction of most adult education theory. This is particularly so in planning theory, because the essential social nature of individual action fails to appear in any meaningful understanding of how to conduct the practice of adult education planning. Out of this pragmatic tradition has developed a more situated (rather than decontextualized) understanding of planning practice. Contemporary philosophical (Bernstein, 1983) and educational (Schwab, 1969) renditions of this viewpoint see social context as a central mediating force (not a nuisance) in understanding human action. In this tradition, the characteristic circumstance faced by planners is a historically and culturally situated one in which conflicts, uncertainties, and several potential courses of action are present (Reid, 1979). Such conflict and uncertainty arise because planners must act in situations deeply embedded in specific organizational and historical conditions that require constant attention and mediation. In Chapters Three, Four, and Five, we show how the planners were aware of and acted upon the conditions particular to their organizational planning circumstances. While we have explored the commonalities in the three cases, each is situated in a unique set of circumstances.

Planners must invariably act in worlds in which the outcomes of their intentions cannot be known with certainty before they embark on specific courses of action. As Dewey and other pragmatists have argued, almost all human action involves the central recognition of an indeterminate situation and the active transformation of it so as to render it determinate (Dewey, 1938). Many life situations are indeterminate because there is no absolutely correct answer for what to do or how to do it. Planning practice, being fundamentally a human social activity, is characterized by the same ambiguity. Often, many alternatives are viable in any given planning situation. As Schön says, professionals do not simply select means to solve clear ends; rather, they must "reconcile, integrate, or choose among conflicting appreciations of a situation so as to construct a problem worth solving" (1983, p. 6). Therefore, because planning is a deeply contextual activity, it is necessarily also typically a contingent activity. Consequently, the important dimension to this depiction of practice is its action component—planners must act, for they do not have the luxury of continual contemplation. But the reason they must act is the essential contingency and situatedness of their daily planning lives. For educational programs to come into being, planners must envision futures (Forester, 1989) for previously indeterminate planning circumstances. That is, given their organizational setting and its location in a historical context, planners must envision and pursue deliberate courses of action in order to create educational programs for adults. The underlying mode of rationality for such action is practical, not scientific.

In order to act in planning situations, planners must make a practical judgment, "a judgement of what to do, or what is to be done: a judgment respecting the future termination of an incomplete and so far indeterminate situation" (Dewey, 1915, p. 514). The contextual and contingent nature of planning means that planners are always choosing what is to be done. But, as we have already argued, planners are not free to do anything; their ability to plan programs depends greatly on what is possible in their particular institutional context, given all its attendant interests and relationships of power. Thus, planners are involved in a practical process of adjudicating alternative courses of action in situations in which few decisions are unassailably right. That is, planners must choose what to do in typically uncertain circumstances. Yet some choices are clearly better than others, depending on the situation. Determining the best course in the given circumstances is a practical process. It is to this formidable task that planners must attend when making judgments about what to do.

Practical Reasoning

The process used by planners in making these choices, called "practical reasoning" by philosophers (Bernstein, 1983; Raz, 1978) and curriculum theorists (Reid, 1979; Schwab, 1969) alike, is continuous in the ways they approach and resolve most everyday problems. The practical reasoning of planning practice is a skilled social process wherein planners identify questions or problems to which they must respond, establish grounds for deciding answers, and choose from among available solutions. Practical reasoning, as we use it here, is a complex social process of determining specific courses of educational action. It is complex because of the contextual essence of human activity; it is social because of the need to negotiate between the multiple interests, which contributes to the indeterminacy of structured yet contingent planning situations. Despite the principled and procedural exhortations of the classical view, we are arguing that planning practice is fundamentally characterized by uncertainty and that planners resolve that uncertainty by using practical reasoning to make judgments about what to do.

As Reid (1979) indicates, central to understanding planning as a practical process is understanding its judgmental nature. Because planning arises from indeterminate circumstances, planners make judgments about what to do. Bernstein describes the judgmental nature of practical reasoning as

> a form of reasoning that is concerned with choice and involves deliberation. It deals with that which is variable and about which there can be differing opinions. It is a type of reasoning in which there is a mediation between general principles and a concrete particular situation that requires choice and deliberation. In forming such a judgement there are no determinate technical rules by which a particular can simply be subsumed under that which is general or universal. What is required is an interpretation and specification of universals that are appropriate to this particular situation [1983, p. 54].

Note the emphasis on the mediation of circumstance and the rejection of generalized principles as guides to action. Practical reasoning challenges the hypothetico-deductive problem-solving process and proposes instead a reasoning process concerned with negotiating about which courses of action to pursue. But Bernstein and Reid also point to the view that the world of the practical often lacks clear and consistent standards by which to know what to do. Indeterminate situations are difficult to resolve precisely because this ambiguity characterizes much human activity. How planners resolve this ambiguity depends on what they value as important, which Usher describes as the essential ethical concern with "how to act rightly in the world" (1991, p. 308). Seeing planning as a process of practical reasoning therefore reveals its essential ethical and human character.

Practical reasoning rejects the perspective of scientific theory being applied instrumentally to practice problems and proposes instead humans acting in practical ways to resolve planning dilemmas in situated and contingent circumstances. This is a view of reasoning proposed long ago by Aristotle in his notion of "phronesis," which is a type of reasoning that has to do with making ethical choices in the discharge of citizenship duties (McKeon, 1947). Seeing practical reasoning as central to planners' actions reveals both the essential ethical and social dimensions of practice. Therefore, to understand planning practice in adult education, we have to understand that it does not follow the comprehensive rationality model of scientific inquiry. Rather, planning practice is fundamentally situated in a context, action-oriented, and practically judgmental. Our effort to depict planning as a practical and contextual activity of negotiating interests is meant to build upon this view of the practical world of adult education.

This depiction of practical reasoning is central to a number of converging works that seek to understand rational human action as practical (Bernstein, 1983; Bright, 1985; Carr and Kemmis, 1986; Kuhn, 1970; Schön, 1983, 1987; Usher, 1991; Usher and Bryant, 1989) and, obviously, is crucial to the characterization of planning portrayed in this book. It gives us a way to understand rational planning action in a practical rather than scientific manner. It is particularly revealing for its insights into the contingency side of Giddens's agency/structure depiction, for this tradition provides a way to conceptualize the indeterminate and judgmental dimensions of planning practice. And, by opening the way for considering the ethical and social dimensions of practice typically ignored in scientific portrayals, it fundamentally provides insight into understanding how interests are crucial to the formation of educational programs. Thus, the practical tradition, in its rejection of scientific rationality, goes a long way toward placing practice in the context of people acting in the real world.

But there is a central issue with which this tradition fails to grapple adequately, and it has to do with Giddens's concern about integrating agency and structure. Simply put, this tradition really does not yet provide an adequate theory of human action. Although it reinvigorates the pragmatic concerns with the social dimensions of human activity and begins to outline the complexity of those dimensions, the practical tradition remains essentially agency centered. Thus, while planners gain important insights regarding the contingency and indeterminacy of human action, the nature and motivation of that human action are only vaguely depicted. Furthermore, it provides only hints of its socially structured dimensions. Specifically, what the tradition fails to provide is an analysis of power that accounts for the social structure of human actions and an understanding of how interests are central to planners' judgments and actions. In other words, this depiction of planning does not illuminate the social and ethical nature of planning or the normative conditions under which it operates. Furthermore, it fails to argue for any particular ethical point of view about whose interests planners should represent and it does not provide an analytical framework for negotiating interests within relationships of power.

Therefore, while the tradition of practical reasoning has been significant in inspiring our analysis and interpretation of planning practice, it does not go far enough in providing a useful guide to program planning because it is not able to adequately depict the situated and structured relationship of the planner to the setting of practice. To that end, we have built our analysis in Part Three on pushing the insights of the practical tradition and coupling them with a more critical and structural tradition (Forester, 1989, 1993; Giddens, 1979, 1984; Isaac, 1987; Lave, 1988) in order to understand more precisely how planners construct programs. In other words, the practical tradition goes a long way toward demystifying the model of scientific rationality and proposing a more people-oriented account of what planning practice is like. But it fails to go much beyond rather vague depictions of practice—and the consequent relationship between theory and practice—as contextual and action oriented; by failing to truly integrate the planner and the

setting, it remains centered on planners' discretion and fails to theo-
rize about the nature of the setting in which the planner acts.
Without such an analysis, how to improve practice is not clear.
While the elements of situation, indeterminacy, judgment, and action are important starting points, we believe this book expands the
traditional theory by proposing an interest-based negotiation process within relationships of power. These elements are needed to
push the boundaries of the practical tradition in order to see
planners' judgments and actions as politically and ethically structured practice.

Integrating Agency and Structure:
Planning as a Social Practice

In order to see planning as practically, rather than comprehensively, rational and to develop the notions of politics and ethics, we
need a more useful understanding of just how individuals are able
to act in the real world. In Chapter Two, we argue that the classical,
naturalistic, and critical theories of planning tend to emphasize
either individual volition or structural determinism, with none able
to provide a heuristically useful understanding of human action in
social settings. The recitation of the cases and their orientation to
planning principles are meant to be our practical solution to that
problem. But it still remains necessary to root those claims in theory. To that end, we seek here to meet the essential challenge of
planning theory today, which is to link structure and agency, that
is, to integrate planning and practical human action with social
settings. We argue that in order to deal with the misleading po-
larism of volition versus determinism, we have to see the fundamental interdependence and situatedness of people acting in social
settings. This argument depends on recognizing that planners are
knowledgeable social actors, that is, they understand their social
settings and are able to act purposefully within them (which leads
to reinvigorating early pragmatic notions). Finally, we argue that
a theory of planning practice must integrate action and structure,
which is why it is useful to see planning as negotiation between and
about interests.

In order to understand the practical nature of planning in

adult education, we have to recognize that such activity is both human and situated (Bernstein, 1983; Giddens, 1979; Lave, 1988); that is, we have to understand planning practice as people acting in social settings. This led us to propose the centrality of politics (Chapter Six) and interests (Chapter Seven) to human action. Traditional planning theories, with their emphases on either self-determination or structural determination, have failed to clarify what Giddens refers to as "the essential recursiveness of social life, as constituted in social practices" (1979, p. 5). *Recursiveness* means that planners are "active social actors, located in time and space, reflexively and recursively acting upon the world in which they live and which they fashion at the same time" (Lave, 1988, p. 8). Planners' actions and the settings in which they act are dialectically structured, a fact that, in turn, forces us to recognize "the partially determined, partially determining character of human agency" (Lave, 1988, p. 16). With this notion, we now are able to understand the effect of human action—agency—on the context of practice—structure—as well as the reverse. In other words, planners neither act in totally unencumbered ways nor is their action completely determined by social structures; setting and action are truly interactive and mutually constitutive. This central idea means that not only are planners able to act out their interests in the world but also that their actions are enabled and constrained by the social norms and the power relationships within the settings in which they plan programs. Practice is thus ethically governed rather than scientifically deductive (Bernstein, 1971, 1976; Giddens, 1979; Kuhn, 1970). Isaac's (1987) depiction of relationships of power as underlying structural capacities exercised contingently on a daily basis is thus central to understanding the social nature of planning. This is also why we draw upon interests and relationships of power to comprehend practice, for they allow us to see the purposefulness of planners' actions—interests—within the context of their actions—relationships of power—and how the two recursively construct programs through negotiation. The notion of recursiveness is thus crucial to our portrayal of planning practice, for this concept allows us to place a knowledgeable planner in a structured setting. This provides the connection left dangling in the practical tradition. That tradition, as depicted in adult education theory, remains agency centered because it depicts the planner as acting in context, rather than the planner's actions both creating, and being created by, the structured nature of social interaction. That is, we provide an account not only of how planners act but of how their action both structures, and is structured by, the organizational context in which they plan programs.

Giddens has elaborated extensively on this "duality of structure" (1979, p. 5), arguing that human activities and their social settings, such as planning practice in adult education, are both the medium and the outcome of social practices. In this view, human action and social setting are not two independent sets of phenomena but actually represent the "dialectical interplay of agency and structure" (Bernstein, 1986, p. 239). We need to explain a key point here, because it is central to understanding how planners can both act in their planning worlds and be acted upon by them. This is the concept of *practical consciousness,* which is "tacit knowledge that is skillfully applied . . . but which the actor is not able to formulate discursively" (Giddens, 1979, p. 57). Bernstein's prosaic rendition of this concept is more insightful: "human agents practically know a great deal about what they are doing, about their society, about the rules of the games [i.e., the "structure" of social settings] in which they find themselves (and even how to get around these rules). Social agents are always reflexively monitoring their action" (1986, p. 241). This notion of knowledgeable planners, capable of being aware of and acting purposefully in structured social settings yet having those conditions both enable and constrain their action, is quite important, because it resolves the inability of scientific planning theory to accurately account for how planners construct adult education programs. In addition, it completes the practical tradition, which situates planners in the real world but fails to provide an interactive account of how planners act in, as well as reconstruct, that context.

Our central thesis throughout this book has been that planning is the negotiation of interests within relationships of power. The underlying framework for making this claim resides in the argument that places planners' actions in the context of personal and institutional interests and power relationships. Most theories of planning practice fail to provide meaningful guides to everyday practice, because their analyses are unable to account for the complexity of social actors in structured settings; that is, they have not accounted for the social recursiveness of interest-laden planners acting knowledgeably but contingently in settings structured by relationships of power. Consequently, any theoretical prescriptions have been necessarily limited to technical injunctions for practice because they assume comprehensive rational action and the hierarchical relationship of theory to practice (this remains true as well in structural accounts in which theoretical analysis takes precedence over human action). Part Three of this book, "Guidelines for Responsible Planning," represents our attempt to provide practical guidance based on more encompassing notions of purposeful yet structured action by planners. In this way, the invocation of a structured yet contingent theory of planning practice reinvigorates central pragmatic notions that are crucial to understanding practical human action. This view places scientific planning models at the technical level rather than at the level of encompassing planner rationality. Therefore, planning is not solely scientific, as the classical viewpoint purports. Nor is it simply a matter of situating the planner within a context, as the naturalistic and practical traditions suggest. Nor does the critical viewpoint provide a complete understanding, with its emphasis on the confluence of structural forces. What is required is a theory of human action that integrates agency and structure. Thus, to understand what planners do, how they know what to do, and how they get it done, planning must be seen as a social practice within which knowledgeable planners are able to responsibly negotiate in order to construct educational programs for adults.

Such a formulation of planning practice suggests a need for a different conceptualization of the relationship of theory and practice in adult education. Thus, in our depiction of the politics and ethics of practice, we have elaborated upon the implications of the pragmatic tradition by linking it to a more insightful, critical, and structural theory of human action to develop a more politically and ethically sensitive account of planning practice. Doing this provides the particulars of how practice is structurally situated within relationships of power and interests, the nature of that resulting structured-yet-contingent action, what the social dimensions of practice look like, and—perhaps most important—what norms can be used to define standards for making judgments in practice. Specifically, we have developed an analysis of power as a structured and enduring social capacity that is inherently contingent because of the everyday practical choices planners make in exercising power. Ethically, we have proposed a substantively democratic planning process of representing people and their interests as a standard by which to gauge the "what for" of practice. Our analysis of planning as a structured-yet-contingent process of negotiating between interests within a context of relationships of power goes partway toward responding to Giddens's challenge to link agency and structure as well as fleshing out the practical tradition that we have drawn upon to understand planning practice.

Meeting the Challenges of Planning Theory

We have written this book because of our profound sense that most planning theories in adult education have provided only the barest notions of what planners actually do. In discussing the intellectual traditions that have inspired this analysis, we have argued for the need to reconstitute the notions of what theory is and what good it is. What, then, is the relationship between theory and practice in adult education planning? If we reject the logic and assumptions of scientifically derived comprehensive rationality and adopt a more humanly attuned view of practical and structured human action, how are we to conceive of the relationship of theory and practice? Here we try to develop an understanding of theory, not as an account of a predictably rational world but as a set of guides and values for what matters and how it is possible to act meaningfully in the precarious everyday planning world. Forester, whose work in urban planning and policy analysis has been so inspirational for us, develops central Habermasian theses in reconstituting a practice- and theory relationship: "Since planning is a value-laden activity whose success or failure has consequences for the society encompassing it, any theory of planning must meet a broader set of requirements than that demanded of theories in the natural or physical sciences. Not only must an account of planning practice be empirically fitting, it must also be both practically appropriate to the settings in which planners work and ethically illuminating, helping planners and citizens understand and assess the ethical and political consequences of various possibilities of action" (1993, pp. 15–16).

Forester draws upon Bernstein, who argues that "there is an internal dialectic in the restructuring of social and political theory: when we work through any one of these moments, we discover how the others are implicated. An adequate social and political theory must be empirical, interpretative, and critical" (1976, p. 235). This is the theoretical and practical structure upon which we have based our analysis. Thus, we conclude with a discussion of why these theoretical criteria make sense for understanding planning practice in adult education.

What does it mean for a theory of planning to be empirically fitting? As we suggest in Chapter One, we have sought a plausible account of planning practice, one that can make sense of the everyday world that planners confront when developing educational programs for adults. In other words, to be empirically grounded, "an account of planning practice must fit the experiences of real planning practice" (Forester, 1993, p. 16). That is, such accounts need to be experientially plausible to the extent that practitioners recognize themselves and their actions in the account. This is, of course, not a claim for statistical validity and reliability. But, in a way suggested by Kuhn's (1970) notion of *paradigm*, theoretical accounts of practice must deal with the puzzles and anomalies left unresolved by competing theories. In this way, we have tried to make sense of the political richness and ethical complexity of planning by situating planners as social actors in a context of interests and power, dimensions either unaccounted for or only partially so in other conceptions of planning practice. By drawing attention to the ethical and political dimensions of planning, we have sought to account for the deficiencies of other theories and to depict practice in such a way that planners not only recognize themselves but can also begin to envision new ways in which to act.

If a theory is to provide such guides for action, it must be practically appropriate or interpretive. One central problem of the hypothetico-deductive view of comprehensive rationality as a model for human action is that it is not practical. It does not speak directly to the working interpretations that planners have of the practical circumstances they encounter daily. To be practically appropriate, theoretical accounts of practice must suggest strategies of action that are both "empirically concrete and practically fitting in the 'real world' of planning organizations and politics" (Forester, 1993, p. 17). Thus, the point of Part Three is to provide practical strategies for acting rationally in a political context (Chapter Six), recognizing and representing interests (Chapter Seven), and negotiating (Chapter Eight). These strategies, then, suggest ways in which planners already account for their actions as well as ways in which they can come to more fully understand their daily worlds so that they can act more concretely in them. If practitioners sense that theorists do not appreciate what planners face daily, the theories will be of little value. By the same token, if theories do not suggest strategic responses to that practical reality, their utility for planners having to act in concrete circumstances is negligible. As Forester says, "Empirically ordering facts about planning is not enough; an account of practice must speak to what those facts mean to planners" (1993, p. 18), which is what it means for a theory to be interpretive and practically appropriate.

Being practical necessarily means taking an ethical stance. As we have continually argued, any planning circumstance is typically replete with multiple possibilities for action, each distinctly reflecting sets of interests in how the world should be different. Likewise, no theory of planning is ethically neutral (Forester, 1989). Even the classical viewpoint in adult education fundamentally argues that planners should plan programs in a comprehensively rational way. In other words, planning theories are inevitably selective in pointing out some things planners should do while ignoring or rejecting other possibilities. But neither can planning theories be expected to specify once and for all a set of rules determining ethical conduct in practice, "for the ethical questions of practical judgment will inevitably arise: 'How, in *this* situation, should I apply this rule?'" (Forester, 1993, p. 18). This is the central difficulty of any rule-based system, an inability to be informative in the vagaries of multiple planning situations. What does it mean for a theory to be ethically illuminating if it does not prescribe rule-generated behavior? Following the lead of Bernstein and Forester, we would claim that an ethically illuminating theory can provide guides (not rules) for action and, more important, justifications for those guides. This is no new claim, for all theories of human action are normatively based. We just wish to emphasize the importance of articulating the justifications for acting in certain ways. Furthermore, theories must place the justifications for ethical action in the historical context of what passes for good practice. Otherwise, vague injunctions to "do good" have no legitimate basis. Pointing out threats to practice that may be anticipated and counteracted is what it means to be ethically illuminating. Such an account does not need to have all the answers but should help planners ask ethically insightful questions that help us resolve those questions in deed.

If theories are going to have value to practice, they must enumerate the conditions that constitute practice, provide practical strategies for rational action, and illuminate the ethical standards that can guide and legitimate our actions in planning. We have used this book to further elaborate the practical tradition, which depicts planning practice as a human social endeavor located in a context of interests and power in which the fundamental activity is one of negotiation rather than application of research-based principles to well-understood practice problems. This fundamentally alters the traditional theory-to-practice relationship in adult education. We no longer envision this relationship in its traditional, hierarchical fashion. As Schön (1983) and others (Bernstein, 1983; Bright, 1985; Carr and Kemmis, 1986; Usher, 1991; Usher and Bryant, 1989) have argued, the world of the practical has its own meaning: "although practical knowledge is a kind of 'knowing how,' it is not an exclusively instrumental or technical know-how but one that is situational, ethical and engaged—characteristics which distinguish the practitioner from the 'technician'" (Usher, 1991, p. 309). Theory in this reconfigured relationship is fundamentally concerned with action in the real world, not just a theoretical depiction of it, and is centrally focused on the political and ethical dimensions of human activity in a social world.

We began this chapter with a concern for the challenges of planning theory. To address those concerns, we have discussed the intellectual foundations of our arguments and proposed a broadened view of the relationship of adult educational planning theory to practice. This argument is meant to provide a more utilitarian, practical, and ethically illuminating notion of how theory can serve our interests in leading to responsible practice. Our fundamental charge in that respect is perhaps best captured by Forester: "It is true, of course, that theories do not solve problems in the world; people do. Nevertheless, good theory is what we need when we get stuck. Theories can help alert us to problems, point us toward strategies of response, remind us of what we care about, or prompt our practical insights into the particular cases we confront" (1989, p. 12). This central insight—people solve problems—is what we have pursued throughout this book. This human focus is central to our theory of planning practice. But, as we have argued, the view of planning we present here is about more than people. In order to meet Giddens's central challenge of locating a meaningful theory of human action in a structured social context, we have placed a socially knowledgeable planner in a world structured by relationships of power. Thus, in order to be responsible planners, we have to understand interests and power as central to our actions as adult educators. But as Forester (1989) wryly notes, a critical theory, even one that meets the instrumental, strategic, and ethical dimensions proposed here, is no panacea; it cannot function as dogma, doctrine, or dictate. It can only remind us of what we care about and how to embody those cares in the daily world of our planning practices. In the end, any theory, even one about planning in adult education, must remain essentially what it is—a human creation that attempts a meaningful interpretation of worldly action. Just so, while we believe our view goes partway toward providing a basis for responsible planning, we have to recognize how our own interests have been central to this endeavor, interests fundamentally concerned with how to understand the complexities of planning responsibly for the education of adults. This concern with responsibility, though, comes from the concern that what really matters is the kind of world planners' programs create. This is why planning matters and why planners should care about doing it responsibly.

References

Apple, M. W. *Education and Power*. New York: Routledge & Kegan Paul, 1982.

Apple, M. W. *Teachers and Texts: A Political Economy of Class and Gender Relations in Education*. New York: Routledge & Kegan Paul, 1986.

Apple, M. W. *Ideology and Curriculum*. (2nd ed.) New York: Routledge & Kegan Paul, 1990.

Apple, M. W. "The Text and Cultural Politics." *Educational Researcher*, 1992, *21*(7), 4–11,19.

Apps, J. W. *Problems in Continuing Education*. San Francisco: Jossey-Bass, 1979.

Atkins, E. "The Deliberative Process: An Analysis from Three Perspectives." *Journal of Curriculum and Supervision*, 1986, *1*(4), 265–293.

Balbus, I. D. "The Concept of Interest in Pluralist and Marxian Analysis." *Politics and Society*, 1971, *1*(2), 151–177.

Barone, T. "Curriculum Platforms and Literature." In J. Gress (ed.), *Curriculum: An Introduction to the Field*. Berkeley, Calif.: McCutchan, 1988.

Beals, R. "American Association for Adult Education." In D. Rowden (ed.), *Handbook of Adult Education*. New York: American Association for Adult Education, 1936.

Beder, H. W. "An Environmental Interaction Model for Agency

Development in Adult Education." *Adult Education,* 1978, *28,* 176-190.

Beder, H. W. (ed.). *Marketing Continuing Education.* New Directions for Adult and Continuing Education, no. 31. San Francisco: Jossey-Bass, 1986.

Benner, P. *From Novice to Expert: Excellence and Power in Clinical Nursing Practice.* Reading, Mass.: Addison-Wesley, 1984.

Bernstein, R. J. *Praxis and Action: Contemporary Philosophies of Human Activity.* Philadelphia: University of Pennsylvania Press, 1971.

Bernstein, R. J. *The Restructuring of Social and Political Theory.* Philadelphia: University of Pennsylvania Press, 1976.

Bernstein, R. J. *Beyond Objectivism and Relativism: Science, Hermeneutics, and Praxis.* Philadelphia: University of Pennsylvania Press, 1983.

Bernstein, R. J. "Structuration as Critical Theory." *Praxis International,* 1986, *6*(2), 235-249.

Beyer, L. E., and Apple, M. W. "Values and Politics in the Curriculum." In L. E. Beyer and M. W. Apple (eds.), *The Curriculum: Problems, Prospects, and Possibilities.* Albany: State University of New York Press, 1988.

Boone, E. J. *Developing Programs in Adult Education.* Englewood Cliffs, N.J.: Prentice-Hall, 1985.

Boyle, P. G. *Planning Better Programs.* New York: McGraw-Hill, 1981.

Bright, B. P. "The Content–Method Relationship in the Study of Adult Education." *Studies in the Education of Adults,* 1985, *17*(2), 168-183.

Bright, B. P. (ed.). *Theory and Practice in the Study of Adult Education: The Epistemological Debate.* New York: Routledge & Kegan Paul, 1989.

Brookfield, S. D. *Understanding and Facilitating Adult Learning: A Comprehensive Analysis of Principles and Effective Practices.* San Francisco: Jossey-Bass, 1986.

Bulbin, J. B. "Update on Employment Law." Paper presented at the 22nd annual conference, Higher Education and the Law, Athens, Georgia, July 1991.

Buskey, J. H. "Utilizing a Systematic Program Planning Process."

In Q. H. Gessner (ed.), *Handbook on Continuing Higher Education*. New York: American Council on Education and Macmillan, 1987.

Caffarella, R. S. *Program Development and Evaluation Resource Book for Trainers*. New York: Wiley, 1988.

Carr, W., and Kemmis, S. *Becoming Critical*. London: Falmer Press, 1986.

Cervero, R. M. "Collaboration in University Continuing Professional Education." In H. W. Beder (ed.), *Realizing the Potential of Interorganizational Cooperation*. New Directions for Continuing Education, no. 23. San Francisco: Jossey-Bass, 1984.

Cervero, R. M. "Becoming More Effective in Everyday Practice." In B. A. Quigley (ed.), *Fulfilling the Promise of Adult and Continuing Education*. New Directions for Adult and Continuing Education, no. 44. San Francisco: Jossey-Bass, 1989.

Collins, M. *Adult Education as Vocation*. New York: Routledge & Kegan Paul, 1991.

Connolly, W. E. "On 'Interests' in Politics." *Politics and Society*, 1972, *2*(4), 459–477.

Cornbleth, C. "Curriculum in and out of Context." *Journal of Curriculum and Supervision*, 1988, *3*(2), 85–96.

Cunningham, P. M. "Making a More Significant Impact on Society." In B. A. Quigley (ed.), *Fulfilling the Promise of Adult and Continuing Education*. New Directions for Adult and Continuing Education, no. 44. San Francisco: Jossey-Bass, 1989.

Dewey, J. "The Logic of Judgments of Practice." *Journal of Philosophy, Psychology, and Scientific Methods*, 1915, *12*, 505–523, 533–543.

Dewey, J. *The Public and Its Problems*. Chicago: Swallow Press, 1927.

Dewey, J. *Logic: The Theory of Inquiry*. Troy, Mo.: Holt, Rinehart & Winston, 1938.

Dominick, J. "How Adult Educators Make Program Development Decisions in Practice." Unpublished doctoral dissertation, Department of Adult Education, University of Georgia, 1990.

Dougherty, M. S. "Adult Educators' Practical Knowledge of Power in Their Organizations." Unpublished doctoral dissertation, Department of Adult Education, University of Georgia, 1990.

Dreyfus, H. L., and Dreyfus, S. E. *Mind over Machine.* Oxford, England: Blackwell, 1986.

Egan, K. "Metaphors in Collision: Objectives, Assembly Lines, and Stories." *Curriculum Inquiry,* 1988, *18*(1), 63–86.

Ellsworth, E. "Why Doesn't This Feel Empowering? Working Through the Myths of Critical Pedagogy." *Harvard Educational Review,* 1989, *59*(3), 297–324.

Forester, J. "Critical Theory and Planning Practice." In J. Forester (ed.), *Critical Theory and Public Life.* Cambridge, Mass.: MIT Press, 1985.

Forester, J. *Planning in the Face of Power.* Berkeley: University of California Press, 1989.

Forester, J. "Evaluation, Ethics, and Traps." In N. Krumholz and J. Forester (eds.), *Making Equity Planning Work: Leadership in the Public Sector.* Philadelphia: Temple University Press, 1990.

Forester, J. *Critical Theory, Public Policy, and Planning Practice.* Albany: State University of New York Press, 1993.

Frankel, C. "John Dewey's Social Philosophy." In S. M. Cahn (ed.), *New Studies in the Philosophy of John Dewey.* Hanover, N.H.: University Press of New England, 1977.

Freedman, L. *Quality in Continuing Education: Principles, Practices, and Standards for Colleges and Universities.* San Francisco: Jossey-Bass, 1987.

Freire, P. *Pedagogy of the Oppressed.* (M. Ramos, trans.) New York: Seabury Press, 1970.

Gessner, Q. H. (ed.). *Handbook on Continuing Higher Education.* New York: American Council on Education and Macmillan, 1987.

Giddens, A. *Central Problems in Social Theory: Action, Structure, and Contradiction in Social Analysis.* Berkeley: University of California Press, 1979.

Giddens, A. *The Constitution of Society.* Berkeley: University of California Press, 1984.

Giroux, H. *Theory and Resistance in Education.* South Hadley, Mass.: Bergin & Garvey, 1983.

Goodson, I. F. "Studying Curriculum: A Social Constructionist Perspective." In I. F. Goodson and R. Walker (eds.), *Biography,*

Identity, and Schooling: Episodes in Educational Research. London: Falmer Press, 1991.

Griffin, C. *Curriculum Theory in Adult and Lifelong Education.* London: Croom Helm, 1983.

Griffith, W. S. "Educational Needs: Definition, Assessment, and Utilization." *School Review,* 1978, *86*(3), 382–294.

Habermas, J. *Knowledge and Human Interests* (J. J. Shapiro, trans.) Portsmouth, N.H.: Heinemann Educational Books, 1971.

Hart, M. U. "Liberation Through Consciousness Raising." In J. Mezirow and Associates, *Fostering Critical Reflection in Adulthood: A Guide to Transformative and Emancipatory Learning.* San Francisco: Jossey-Bass, 1990.

Hart, M. U. *Adult Education and the Future of Work.* New York: Routledge & Kegan Paul, 1992.

Hawkesworth, M. "Knowers, Knowing, and Known: Feminist Theory and Claims of Truth." *Signs: Journal of Women in Culture and Society,* 1989, *14*(3), 533–557.

Houle, C. O. "An Unparalleled Experiment in Adult Education." In M. Ely (ed.), *Handbook of Adult Education.* New York: Institute of Adult Education, Columbia University, 1948.

Houle, C. O. "The Education of Adult Educational Leaders." In M. Knowles (ed.), *Handbook of Adult Education in the United States.* Chicago: Adult Education Association of the U.S.A., 1960.

Houle, C. O. *The Design of Education.* San Francisco: Jossey-Bass, 1972.

Houle, C. O. *Continuing Learning in the Professions.* San Francisco: Jossey-Bass, 1980.

Ilsley, P. J. *Improving Conference Design and Outcomes.* New Directions for Adult and Continuing Education, no. 28. San Francisco: Jossey-Bass, 1985.

Isaac, J. C. *Power and Marxist Theory: A Realist View.* Ithaca, N.Y.: Cornell University Press, 1987.

Knowles, M. S. *Informal Adult Education.* New York: Association Press, 1950.

Knowles, M. S. *The Modern Practice of Adult Education: From Pedagogy to Andragogy.* (2nd ed.) New York: Cambridge Books, 1980.

Knox, A. B. *Enhancing Proficiencies of Continuing Educators.*

New Directions for Continuing Education, no. 1. San Francisco: Jossey-Bass, 1979.

Knox, A. B. (ed.). *Leadership Strategies for Meeting New Challenges.* New Directions for Continuing Education, no. 13. San Francisco: Jossey-Bass, 1982.

Knox, A. B. *Helping Adults Learn: A Guide to Planning, Implementing, and Conducting Programs.* San Francisco: Jossey-Bass, 1986.

Knox, A. B. and Associates. *Developing, Administering, and Evaluating Adult Education.* San Francisco: Jossey-Bass, 1980.

Kowalski, T. J. *The Organization and Planning of Adult Education.* Albany: State University of New York Press, 1988.

Kuhn, T. S. *The Structure of Scientific Revolutions.* (2nd. ed.) Chicago: University of Chicago Press, 1970.

Langenbach, M. *Curriculum Models in Adult Education.* Malabar, Fla.: Krieger, 1988.

Lave, J. *Cognition in Practice.* Cambridge, England: Cambridge University Press, 1988.

Lewis, C. H., and Dunlop, C. C. "Successful and Unsuccessful Adult Education Programs." In T. J. Sork (ed.), *Mistakes Made and Lessons Learned: Overcoming Obstacles to Successful Program Planning.* New Directions for Adult and Continuing Education, no. 49. San Francisco: Jossey-Bass, 1991.

Lewis, L. H. (ed.). *Experiential and Simulation Techniques for Teaching Adults.* New Directions for Continuing Education, no. 30. San Francisco: Jossey-Bass, 1986.

Long, H. "Experimental Research." In H. Long and R. Hiemstra (eds.), *Changing Approaches to Studying Adult Education.* San Francisco: Jossey-Bass, 1980.

Long, H. "Evolution of a Formal Knowledge Base." In J. Peters, P. Jarvis, and Associates (eds.), *Adult Education: Evolution and Achievements in a Developing Field of Study.* San Francisco: Jossey-Bass, 1991.

McKeon, R. *Introduction to Aristotle.* Chicago: University of Chicago Press, 1947.

March, J., and Simon, H. *Organizations.* New York: Wiley, 1958.

Mehan, H. "Institutional Decision Making." In B. Rogoff and J.

Lave (eds.), *Everyday Cognition: Its Development in Social Context.* Cambridge, Mass.: Harvard University Press, 1984.

Millar, C. "Educating the Educators of Adults: Two Cheers for Curriculum Negotiation." *Journal of Curriculum Studies,* 1989, *21*(2), 161–168.

Morgan, G. *Images of Organization.* Newbury Park, Calif.: Sage, 1986.

Nadler, L. L. *Designing Training Programs: The Critical Events Model.* Reading, Mass.: Addison-Wesley, 1982.

Nadler, L., and Nadler, Z. *The Comprehensive Guide to Successful Conferences and Meetings.* San Francisco: Jossey-Bass, 1987.

Nowlen, P. M. *A New Approach to Continuing Education for Business and the Professions: The Performance Model.* New York: Macmillan, 1988.

Pennington, F., and Green, J. "Comparative Analysis of Program Development in Six Professions." *Adult Education,* 1976, *27*, 13–23.

Perrow, C. *Complex Organizations: A Critical Essay.* Glenview, Ill.: Scott, Foresman, 1972.

Pinar, W. F., and Bowers, C. A. "Politics of Curriculum: Origins, Controversies, and Significance of Critical Perspectives." In G. Grant (ed.), *Review of Research in Education, 18.* Washington, D.C.: American Educational Research Association, 1992.

Pittman, V. "Some Things Practitioners Wish Adult Education Professors Would Teach." *Adult Learning,* 1989, *1*(3), 30.

Posner, G. J. "Models of Curriculum Planning." In L. E. Beyer and M. W. Apple (eds.), *The Curriculum: Problems, Prospects, and Possibilities.* Albany: State University of New York Press, 1988.

Pusey, M. *Jurgen Habermas.* London: Tavistock Publications, 1987.

Raz, J. (ed.). *Practical Reasoning.* Oxford, England: Oxford University Press, 1978.

Reid, W. A. "Practical Reasoning and Curriculum Theory: In Search of a New Paradigm." *Curriculum Inquiry,* 1979, *9*, 187–207.

Rogoff, B. "Introduction: Thinking and Learning in the Social Context." In B. Rogoff and J. Lave (eds.), *Everyday Cognition:*

Its Development in Social Context. Cambridge, Mass.: Harvard University Press, 1984.

Rosenblum, S. H. *Involving Adults in the Educational Process.* New Directions for Continuing Education, no. 26. San Francisco: Jossey-Bass, 1985.

Rubenson, K. "Adult Education Research: In Quest of a Map of the Territory." *Adult Education,* 1982, *32*(2), 57–74.

Schmidt, W., and Svenson, E. "Methods in Adult Education." In M. Knowles (ed.), *Handbook of Adult Education in the United States.* Chicago: Adult Education Association of the U.S.A., 1960.

Schön, D. A. *The Reflective Practitioner.* New York: Basic Books, 1983.

Schön, D. A. *Educating the Reflective Practitioner: Toward a New Design for Teaching and Learning in the Professions.* San Francisco: Jossey-Bass, 1987.

Schön, D. A. (ed.). *The Reflective Turn: Case Studies in and on Educational Practice.* New York: Teachers College Press, 1991.

Schubert, W. H. *Curriculum: Perspective, Paradigm, and Possibility.* New York: Macmillan, 1986.

Schwab, J. J. "The Practical: A Language for Curriculum." *School Review,* 1969, *78*(1), 1–24.

Shor, I., and Freire, P. "What Is the 'Dialogical Method' of Teaching?" *Journal of Education,* 1987, *169,* 11–31.

Shulman, L. S. "Knowledge and Teaching: Foundations of the New Reform." *Harvard Educational Review,* 1987, *57*(1), 1–22.

Simerly, R. G., and Associates. *Strategic Planning and Leadership in Continuing Education: Enhancing Organizational Vitality, Responsiveness, and Identity.* San Francisco: Jossey-Bass, 1987.

Simerly, R. G. and Associates. *Handbook of Marketing for Continuing Education.* San Francisco: Jossey-Bass, 1989.

Sork, T. J. (ed.). *Designing and Implementing Effective Workshops.* New Directions for Adult and Continuing Education, no. 22. San Francisco: Jossey-Bass, 1984.

Sork, T. J. (ed.). *Mistakes Made and Lessons Learned: Overcoming Obstacles to Successful Program Planning.* New Directions for Adult and Continuing Education, no. 49. San Francisco: Jossey-Bass, 1991.

Sork, T. J., and Buskey, J. H. "A Descriptive and Evaluative Analysis of Program Planning Literature, 1950–1983." *Adult Education Quarterly*, 1986, *36*, 86–96.

Sork, T. J., and Caffarella, R. S. "Planning Programs for Adults." In S. B. Merriam and P. M. Cunningham (eds.), *Handbook of Adult and Continuing Education*. San Francisco: Jossey-Bass, 1989.

Taba, H. *Curriculum Development: Theory and Practice*. Orlando, Fla.: Harcourt Brace Jovanovich, 1962.

Tierney, W. G. "Empowering or Not Empowering? Continuing Debate over Non-Repressive Pedagogies." *Harvard Educational Review*, 1990, *60*(3), 390–392.

Tyler, R. W. *Basic Principles of Curriculum and Instruction*. Chicago: University of Chicago Press, 1949.

Usher, R. "Theory and Metatheory in the Adult Education Curriculum." *International Journal of Lifelong Education*, 1991, *10*(4), 305–315.

Usher, R., and Bryant, I. *Adult Education as Theory, Practice, and Research: The Captive Triangle*. New York: Routledge & Kegan Paul, 1989.

Walker, D. F. "A Naturalistic Model for Curriculum Development." *School Review*, 1971, *80*, 51–65.

Walker, D. F. "Curriculum Development in an Art Project." In W. Reid and D. F. Walker (eds.), *Case Studies in Curriculum Change: Great Britain and the United States*. New York: Routledge & Kegan Paul, 1975.

Walker, D. F, and Soltis, J. F. *Curriculum and Aims*. (2nd ed.). New York: Teachers College Press, 1992.

Welton, M. " 'Vivisecting the Nightingale': Reflections on Adult Education as an Object of Study." *Studies in the Education of Adults*, 1987, *19*(1), 46–68.

West, C. *The American Evasion of Philosophy: A Genealogy of Pragmatism*. Madison: University of Wisconsin Press, 1989.

Wilson, A. L. "Science and the Professionalization of American Adult Education, 1934–1989: A Study of Knowledge Development in the Adult Education Handbooks." In A. Blunt (ed.), *Proceedings of the 33rd Annual Adult Education Research Conference*, Saskatoon, Saskatchewan, Canada, 1992.

Index

A

Adult education. *See* Planning practice
Affected public. *See* Legitimate representatives of interests
Agency, 182-185. *See also* Integrating planner discretion and structural constraint
Ambiguity. *See* Uncertainty
Andragogy, 118, 141-142
Anticipating relations of power. *See* Power
Apple, M. W., 8, 21-24, 119, 140-141
Apps, J. W., 3, 14
Aristotle, 181
Atkins, E., 8
Audience, 5-6, 9, 28, 30, 131, 135, 138, 145, 164, 189. *See also* Negotiating
Authority, 122, 132, 147, 166, 168. *See also* Power

B

Balbus, L. D., 124
Bargaining. *See* planning strategies
Barone, T., 26

Beals, R., 172, 175
Beder, H. W., 160, 169
Benner, P., 8
Bernstein, R. J., 8, 27, 173, 176, 178-181, 184-185, 188-190
Beyer, L. E., 8, 21-23, 140
Boone, E. J., 14
Bounded Rationality Cells, 1-4, 128, 131-135. *See also* Rationality
Bowers, C. A., 22
Boyle, P. G., 143, 162, 164-166, 169
Bright, B. P., 172, 176, 181, 190
Brookfield, S. D., 7, 14, 16, 19-20, 118, 166, 168, 175
Bryant, I., 7, 172, 174, 176, 181, 190
Bulbin, J. B., 91
Buskey, J. H., 14, 143, 166-167, 175

C

Caffarella, R. S., 7, 16, 117, 166, 169, 175
Carr, W., 13, 21, 29, 174, 181, 190
Cases of planning practice, 9-11, 33-34; Fixing an Organization through Management Education, 35-61; Promoting Social Change in Community-Based

Education, 88–113; Updating Practitioners in Continuing Education, 62–87
Cervero, R. M., 28, 160, 172
Classical viewpoint. *See* Planning theory
Collins, M., 140
Conflict. *See* Negotiation
Connolly, W. E., 124
Consciousness-raising, 22
Consensus. *See* Negotiation
Constructing and reconstructing relationships of power and interests, 30, 126, 136, 142, 158–164, 167, 170. *See also* Interests; Negotiating; Planning practice
Content, 4–6, 9, 17, 21, 28, 30, 138, 145, 164, 169. *See also* Negotiating
Context, 12, 17–21, 25–28, 30, 118–119, 128–129, 131, 135–136, 142, 162, 165–167, 172, 177, 181–182, 184–185, 190
Cornbleth, C., 8
Counteracting. *See* Planning strategies
Critical pedagogy, 22–24
Critical social theory, 8, 22, 125, 129
Critical viewpoint. *See* Planning theory
Cunningham, P. M., 22
Curriculum. *See* Content

D

Decision-making, 18–21, 25, 143, 166
Deliberation, 6, 18, 19–21, 25–26, 140, 154, 180; as making choices, 18–20, 140, 180, 187. *See also* Judgments; Negotiation; Naturalistic viewpoint
Democracy, 5, 23–24. *See also* Substantively democratic planning
Democratic planning. *See* Substantively democratic planning
Descartes, R., 175
Dewey, J., 126, 140, 177–179

Domination, 24, 29, 121–122. *See also* Power
Dominick, J., 20, 166
Dougherty, S. M., 166
Dreyfus, H. L., 8
Dreyfus, S. E., 8
Dunlop, C. C., 166

E

Egan, K., 26
Ellsworth, E., 23–24, 118
Emancipation, 21, 23
Ethics, 6, 11, 20–21, 23–25, 124, 137–138, 182–183, 186; as instructive for practice, 138–141, 153, 189; standards of, 20, 22, 32, 115–116, 142, 164–165, 181, 187; as thinking, 137, 153. *See also* Planners' knowledge; Planning responsibly; Substantively democratic planning
Evaluation, 3, 17, 20

F

Forester, J., 4, 8, 11, 13, 23, 25–27, 31, 118, 121, 125, 127–135, 137–138, 141–142, 149, 153, 156, 159–160, 162, 165, 168, 173–174, 179, 182, 187–189, 191
Format, 4–6, 9, 17, 20, 28, 31–32, 138, 145, 164, 169. *See also* Negotiating
Frankel, J., 140
Freedman, L., 169
Freire, P., 22

G

Gessner, Q. H., 169
Giddens, A., 119, 121, 172, 176, 181–182, 184–185, 187, 191
Giroux, H., 21–22, 140–141
Goodson, I. F., 13, 26–28
Green, J., 15
Griffin, C., 8, 22
Griffith, W. S., 139, 143

H

Habermas, J., 21, 29, 162, 173–174, 176, 187
Hart, M. U., 8, 22, 140
Hawkesworth, M., 27
Hegemony, 22
Houle, C. O., 15, 18–19, 118, 169, 173, 175

I

Ilsley, P. J., 169
Indeterminate, 21, 177–183
Individual discretion and structural constraint. See Integrating planner discretion and structural constraint
Institutional leadership. See Legitimate representatives of interests
Institutional setting. See Organizational context
Integrating planner discretion and structural constraint (agency and structure), 13, 25–30, 116, 118, 171–173, 176–177, 181–187, 191
Interests, 1, 4–6, 9, 11–13, 16, 21–22, 25, 27–32, 117–119, 129, 131–135, 143–144, 153, 163–164, 171–172, 177, 179, 182, 184, 186, 188–191; anticipating, 6, 30–31, 117, 128, 167; as causally related to the construction of programs, 4–5, 9, 28, 30–33, 123, 138, 140, 142, 148, 150, 156, 171, 181–182; definition of, 29, 122–123; and the exercise of power, 119–120, 122–124, 138; expressed, 124–126, 138, 140, 143, 146–147, 149–150, 159, 164; ideal, 124–126, 140–142, 148, 164; and Fixing an Organization Through Management Education, 34, 43–47, 60–61; and Promoting Social Change in Community-Based Education, 34, 95–99, 111–113; real, 125–126, 138, 140, 142–143, 146–147, 159, 164; representing, democrati-

cally, 137–143; and Updating Practitioners in Continuing Education, 34, 69–74, 86–87. See also Negotiating; Negotiation; Legitimate representatives of interests
Isaac, J. C., 8, 29, 119–126, 142, 172–173, 176, 182, 184

J

Judgments, 4, 6, 8, 11, 17–21, 24–25, 30, 32, 130–131, 138–139, 143–145, 147, 149, 157, 160, 164, 167–169, 179–183, 187. See also Deliberation
Justifying choices, 18, 20, 189–190. See also Deliberation

K

Kemmis, S., 13, 21, 29, 174, 176, 181, 190
Knowles, M. S., 14–15, 118, 141, 173
Knox, A. B., 14, 17–19, 131, 139, 143, 166, 169
Kowalski, T. J., 143, 165–166, 169
Kuhn, T. S., 181, 184, 188

L

Langenbach, M., 14
Lave, J., 8, 27–28, 172, 182, 184
Learners. See Legitimate representatives of interests
Legitimate representatives of interests, 5, 31, 116, 134, 142–143, 153–155; affected public as, 151–153; institutional leadership as, 149–151; learners as, 143–146, 157; planners as, 147–148; teachers as, 146–147. See also Interests; Substantively democratic planning
Lewis, C. H., 166
Lewis, L. H., 169
Long, H., 173, 176

M

McKeon, R., 181
March, J., 131
Mehan, H., 174
Millar, C., 7
Morgan, G., 29, 123

N

Nadler, L. L., 169
Nadler, Z., 69
Naturalistic viewpoint. *See* Planning theory
Negotiating, 4-6, 12-13, 25, 27-28, 131-135, 157; about audience, 49-53, 75-77, 101-104; between interests, 29-30, 137-138, 147, 153, 155, 157-158, 160-161, 163, 167, 180, 183, 187; as the central activity of planning, 4-6, 11, 13, 29, 31, 33, 116, 155-156, 160-161, 170, 191; about content, 54-56, 77-80, 104-106; about format, 56-60, 80-86, 106-111; about interests, 30, 32, 155, 180-183; with interests, 29; about purpose, 47-49, 74-75, 99-101; responsibly, 140, 162. *See also* Interests
Negotiating interests and power, 1, 4-6, 12-13, 28-32, 115-116, 118, 126-127, 137, 153, 155, 159, 170-171, 181-182, 184-185, 190-191. *See also* Interests; Negotiating; Power
Negotiation, 13, 28-31, 121-122, 166; conflict in, 31, 47, 52, 84-85, 115, 121, 129-130, 133-134, 147, 151, 157; consensus about, 31-32, 60, 74-75, 84, 86, 100-102, 121, 127, 129-133, 145-146, 156-157
Networking. *See* Planning strategies
Noise, 3-4, 31, 128. *See also* Planning practice; Politics of planning
Nowlen, P. M., 70

O

Organizational context, 3-4, 16, 19, 21, 25, 27-29, 115, 117-118, 125, 127, 131-132, 149, 162, 179. *See also* Rationality
Organizational relations of power. *See* Power

P

Peirce, C. S., 177
Pennington, F., 15
Perrow, C., 131
Pinar, W. F., 22
Pittman, V., 6
Planner action, 5, 26, 117, 119, 172, 177
Planner discretion and structural constraint. *See* Integrating planner discretion and structural constraint
Planners, 6, 9-11, 14-25, 31-32, 115, 117-118, 122, 125, 135, 143, 147-148, 150, 161-170, 187, 189. *See also* Interests; Legitimate representatives of interests
Planners' knowledge and skills, 116, 161-163; ethical, 163-165; political, 165-167; technical, 167-170
Planning practice, 4, 8-9, 11-13, 18, 20-21, 24-27, 31, 119, 125, 139, 148, 162, 171-173, 188, 191; as acting politically, 23, 31, 117, 127, 156, 158-161; as applied science, 116, 172-177, 179, 185-186, 190; as design, 19, 155-156, 162; as ethically illuminated, 11, 153, 155, 164, 170, 173, 186, 188-190; as making the world different, 3, 5, 138-139, 151, 163, 171, 189, 191; as politically astute, 5, 11, 144, 155, 165, 167, 170, 186, 188; as practical, 1, 3, 173, 177-183, 187; as a social activity, 4, 6, 12, 24, 27-28, 31, 117, 126, 155-156; as socially constructed, 28, 155-157; as a social practice, 116, 171-172, 186
Planning principles, 3-4, 6-7, 26; as applied to practice problems, 14, 16-18
Planning responsibly, 4-5, 11, 127-131, 134-135, 137-138, 140-143,

158, 161–169, 186, 191; as anticipating power and interests, 6,
31–32, 115–117, 119, 129–130,
135–136, 142, 153. *See also* Interests; Negotiating; Power
Planning strategies, 15, 128, 130; of
bargaining, 122, 134–135; of
counteracting, 135; of networking, 132–135, 166; of satisficing,
131–132, 135
Planning theory, 4, 6–8, 22–23, 28,
117–118, 153, 177–178, 187, 190;
classical viewpoint, 3, 14–17, 25–
26, 118, 128, 130–131, 138, 161–
162, 171, 175–176, 180, 183, 186,
189; critical viewpoint, 21–25,
27, 118, 125, 171, 176, 183, 186;
as a guide to action, 11, 16, 139–
140, 158, 162, 180, 182, 185–186,
188–190; naturalistic viewpoint,
17–21, 26–27, 118, 128, 171, 176,
183, 186; as practical, 4, 8, 153,
162; as technical procedures, 4,
21, 160, 167–170, 174, 186
Pluralist conflict, 128, 133–134. *See
also* Power; Rationality
Political boundedness. *See* Power;
Rationality
Politics of planning, 1, 5–7, 11, 16,
21–25, 31, 115, 117–136, 137, 140,
142, 147, 153, 160, 162–163, 165–
168, 183, 186–188
Posner, G. J., 14, 26
Power, 1, 4–5, 8, 11, 17, 21–22, 25,
28–31, 46, 52–53, 61, 117–137,
139–142, 144, 147–148, 153–154,
157–158, 162–165, 167, 170–173,
177, 179, 182, 184, 186–188, 190–
191; anticipating and interpreting relationships of, 115, 117,
120, 127–130, 135, 167; as capacity to act, 29, 119–121, 123, 158;
as constraint to action, 29, 128–
129; contingent exercise of, 119–
124, 128–129, 187; as enduring
social relationships, 29, 119–120,
158, 187; interpersonal relationships of, 6, 22, 25, 144; as legitimate or illegitimate, 122;
maintaining or transforming the
structure of, 122, 126, 136, 159–
161, 165; negotiating as the exercise of, 119, 121–122, 124, 158,
165; organizational relationships
of, 6, 22, 24–25, 29, 44, 51, 115,
144, 147; as reciprocal relationships, 121–122; as socially organized and distributed, 5, 8, 29,
118–119, 123, 172, 187; source of,
as socially ad hoc, 128–129, 131,
133–134; source of, as socially
systematic, 128–129, 133–134,
147; symmetrical and asymmetrical distribution of, 121–122,
127, 129, 133–135, 140–141, 143,
149; ubiquitous nature of, 119;
unequal relationships of, 20–21,
122, 144. *See also* Interests;
Negotiating
Practical consciousness, 185
Practical human action, 8, 20–21,
171–173, 178, 181–182, 186. *See
also* Judgments; Rationality
Practical judgments. *See* Judg-
ments; Rationality
Practical knowledge, 11, 17, 19
Practical reasoning. *See* Rationality
Practical theorists, 19, 172
Practitioners, 7–8, 17, 174, 189
Pragmatics with vision, 115, 141–
143, 153–154
Pragmatism, 138, 177–178, 182, 186
Problem solving, 3, 18, 173, 175,
180, 191
Professionalization, 173, 176
Program planning. *See* Planning
practice; Planning strategies;
Planning theory
Programs. *See* Interests
Purpose, 4–6, 9, 17, 20, 28, 30, 138,
145, 164, 169. *See also*
Negotiating
Pusey, M., 141

R

Rational action, 118, 126–128, 173,
176–177, 181, 190
Rationality: as bounded, 26, 117–
118, 127–136; as political, 128–

129, 135; as practical reasoning,
18, 20-21, 172, 177-183; as scien-
tific, 172-174, 181-182, 185-186;
as unbounded or comprehen-
sive, 26, 118, 130, 162, 173-177,
181, 186-189
Raz, J., 179
Recursiveness, 172, 184-186
Reid, W. A., 18, 21, 178-180
Reproduction, 22, 51, 126, 136, 159.
See also Constructing and recon-
structing relationships of power
and interests
Research methodology, 8-11
Responsibility, 4-5, 158
Rogoff, B., 177
Roles of planners, 4, 170
Rosenblum, S. H., 169
Rubenson, K., 176

S

Satisficing. *See* Planning strategies
Schmidt, W., 174
Schön, D. A., 3, 172-175, 178, 181,
190
Schubert, W. H., 13-14
Schwab, J. J., 7, 18, 143, 178, 179
Shor, I., 22
Shulman, L. S., 8
Simerly, R. G., 166-167, 169
Simon, H., 131
Social change, 9, 22-23, 93, 95-97,
100-101, 103, 105, 107, 109, 112,
149-150, 152
Social context, 3-4, 6, 28-31, 117,
172-173, 178, 185
Social differentiation/division of
labor, 132, 147. *See also* Power;
Rationality
Social justice, 22-24
Social structure, 8, 27, 182. *See also*
Integrating planner discretion
and structural constraint
Sork, T. J., 7, 14, 16, 117, 166, 169,
175
Stakeholders. *See* Interests; Legiti-
mate representatives of interests;

Substantively democratic
planning
Structural constraints, 182-184. *See
also* Integrating planner discretion and structural constraint
Substantively democratic planning,
5, 115, 125, 127, 148, 153-154,
164-165, 187; nurturing of, 129-
130, 133-135, 139-142, 163, 167.
See also Interests
Svenson, E., 174

T

Taba, H., 14
Teachers. *See* Legitimate represen-
tatives of interests
Technical procedures. *See* Plan-
ning theory
Theory and practice relationships,
173-177, 182, 186, 187-191
Theory-in-practice, 175
Theory of human action, 27, 172,
176-179, 182-183, 186, 190-191.
See also Planner action;
Rationality
Tierney, W. G., 23
Tyler, R. W., 14-17, 20, 26, 163, 175

U

Uncertainty, 20-21, 31, 143, 178-
181
Update Model of continuing education, 65, 67-71, 75, 77, 79, 81, 83,
85, 157
Usher, R., 7, 172, 174, 176, 181, 190

V

Values, 6, 11, 16-20, 23, 30, 122,
137, 139, 149, 163-164, 181, 187

W

Walker, D. F., 13, 16, 18, 26
Welton, M., 8, 22
West, C., 140
Wilson, A. L., 175